PLAY & LEARN

WITH YOUR BABY

SIMPLE ACTIVITIES WITH AMAZING BENEFITS

PLAY & LEARN

WITH YOUR BABY

SIMPLE ACTIVITIES WITH AMAZING BENEFITS

Contents

It's been a few years since my kids were babies, but I have to confess that when they were little, I didn't really tap into baby clubs. I lived in my family bubble and assumed that clubs weren't that beneficial. How wrong I was! It's only now, having led and studied baby groups, that I appreciate their enormous benefits.

In The Baby Club we sing songs, discover through play and share stories, but there are lots of other things going on under the surface. In fact, I was so amazed by the impact of simple activities on development and bonding that I decided to take a course to be a Peep practitioner – qualified to deliver the Learning Together Programme developed by the charity, Peeple.

My training highlighted how everyday activities are great opportunities for a baby to learn, without the need for expensive toys – there's a world of discovery in everyday items and simple toys. I was amazed that just playing with a ball introduces ideas such as turn-taking, and that blowing bubbles helps babies build the muscles needed for talking – how cool is that?!

That's why this book is so useful. There are lots of activities to enjoy with your baby with explanations for why they're so helpful. When you understand the potential behind the simplest of activities, you start to see how every task, meal, changing session or buggy ride becomes an opportunity to bond, encourage or aid your baby's understanding of the world.

Hopefully, trying some activities will build your confidence in your own parenting skills. You probably already do some activities without realizing how incredible they are. I also hope this book will give you new ideas for playing, interacting and bonding with your little one. Do share what you learn with friends, family and other parents because the more people who understand the benefits of play, the better off all of our children will be.
Enjoy!

Nigel

Nigel Clarke, Presenter at CBeebies' **The Baby Club**

Enjoying this book

Play and Learn with your Baby follows the format of The Baby Club TV show. The book is packed with ideas for playing and interacting with your baby and explains the many developmental benefits of each fun interaction.

- Dip into the "What's in the Bag?" chapter for play ideas using simple household objects and toys.

- Use the tips in Story time to help you share the joy of reading with your baby.

- Enjoy a sing-along in the Song time chapter.

- When out and about, be inspired by the ideas in the Opportunities pages to help your baby notice and learn from the world around them.

Whether it's just the two of you, or a gathering with friends and their babies, enjoy your own baby club experience!

66 Going to a baby club has helped our little one to interact and develop lots of new skills. We play and learn together. 99

Billie's mum, Natalie

HELLO

Learning
through saying hello

Everyone is welcome at The Baby Club and The Hello Song on page 15 is part of the routine. Babies can be quick to learn and soon begin to recognise what comes next, which helps them to feel safe and secure. Routines are also reassuring for adults visiting a baby club. As faces, names and activities become more familiar, joining in with the group becomes less daunting.

Join in with The Hello Song. Be sure to include your baby's name when the time comes, so that your baby feels included and valued. Their name is special to you and it quickly becomes important to them, too.

Your baby's name

A SENSE OF IDENTITY ... It takes time for babies to become aware that they exist separately from you and have their own unique identity. Our name is an essential part of our sense of identity and is often the first word that children want to write. Even the first letter of a name can be special. Singing your baby's name during The Hello Song is a great way to help your baby begin to shape a sense of who they are.

FEELING VALUED ... It is very engaging for your baby when you use their name in playful and positive ways. It helps your baby to feel valued and loved. Try substituting your baby's name into other songs you sing together. You can have fun pointing out the first letter of your baby's name on signs and posters and toddlers love to be the star of made-up stories.

A sense of order

PREDICTABLE ROUTINES ... Routines such as The Hello Song at The Baby Club are valuable as they help babies and toddlers learn about patterns and predict what is going to happen next – this is actually the first stage of mathematical thinking! Incorporate songs, rhymes and activities into existing routines at home, too, perhaps when getting ready to go out or around bath time and bedtime.

LEARNING TO ANTICIPATE ... When you watch your baby carefully, you will recognise how they react to something new and how their behaviour changes when they know what is coming next. When you regularly sing The Hello Song, your baby may get excited, waving their arms or clapping or gurgling. Your baby might also become quiet with anticipation when they know their name is about to be sung!

Saying "Hello"

The Hello Song can also be a fun way to introduce your baby to social situations with friends and family. Learning to say hello encourages your baby to be sociable.

BODY LANGUAGE ... Think about your body language as you sing. Let your baby know you are glad to be with them with a cuddle or a smile and show that you are pleased to see friends, family or even guest teddies. Your baby is watching and ready to learn from your reactions to new people and experiences.

SPEAK OR SING CLEARLY ... The Hello Song has a regular rhythm and lots of rhymes. Emphasise these as you sing or speak to help your baby learn the song and anticipate what is coming next. If your baby is very young or is feeling particularly cuddly, try looking into their eyes and smiling as you sing to reassure them. Try using exaggerated expressions, too. Your baby loves watching your face and will be delighted to see your big smile.

INTERACT ... Notice your baby's responses. If they smile, gurgle or blow bubbles, stop to show you've noticed, then smile back. This interaction models the art of turn-taking in conversations.

USE EMPHASIS ... Emphasise your baby's name when saying hello. This reinforces the importance of their name and helps them to feel loved and valued.

The Hello Song

Hello Christopher

let's all have some fun.

Hello Bonnie

our baby club's begun!

Hello Patel

it's nice to meet all of you!

Hello Gracie

and hello Baby Bear, too!

Hello Connor

join in with our song.

Hello Asha

hello everyone!

**Welcome to The Baby Club,
we're so glad you've come to play**

Hello (your baby's name)

it's going to be a wonderful day!

Dhilan

SING HELLO
Sing to The Baby Club's
tune or your own tune,
adding the names of
the babies at the club,
or family's, friend's, or
soft toys' names.

Millana

Tom

WHAT'S IN THE BAG?

Learning
through everyday play

The Baby Club game "What's in the bag?" provides endless opportunities for warm, sensitive interactions and for making stimulating discoveries with your baby. Each time your baby sees, smells, touches, hears or tastes something new, vital connections are formed in their brain. Hiding a toy or everyday object in a bag and giving your baby time to discover and explore it, stimulates all of your baby's senses. Use the ideas throughout this chapter to help your baby explore, learn and enjoy social interactions.

Let's play...

Before you begin to play What's In The Bag?, follow these tips to help you both get the most from this activity.

1 **SIT ...** Sit in a safe, comfortable space together, giving your baby as much freedom as possible to handle the object and move around. Try keeping your baby's toes bare – babies love to explore with their feet as well as with their hands.

2 **STAY SAFE ...** Make sure the object is clean and safe for your baby to play with, with no sharp edges or small parts that could break off and be swallowed.

3 **EXPLORE ...** Let your baby explore with all their senses. In particular, babies love to explore with their mouths. Your baby's gums and tongue are very sensitive and tell them a lot about how an object feels, smells, and tastes. Exploring this way also strengthens the mouth muscles needed for speech.

4 **WATCH ...** Try not to direct play. Your baby is naturally curious and will feel safe and secure to explore with you close by giving them your quiet attention.

5 **REASSURE ...** Follow your baby's cues. If they appear unsure, give a smile or encouraging word. If your baby holds out an object, or drops it and looks for your reaction, take it, saying thank you. You could have a similar object to explore alongside your baby.

6 **STOP ...** Don't worry if your baby isn't interested. Stay tuned in to your baby's feelings and try returning to the activity later.

Time to play

Early play, with gentle encouragement and reassurance from you, nurtures curiosity, confidence and self-esteem. It even helps your baby begin to manage their emotions. The chance to explore everyday objects gives your baby the skills needed to gain independence.

Physical

BIG AND SMALL MOVEMENTS ... Physically exploring objects strengthens muscles and helps your baby discover how to control and coordinate their body. Your baby gains control of the larger, "gross motor" movements of the head, body and limbs first, then learns to control the smaller, "fine motor" movements of their hands, feet and fingers. Mastering these skills and learning how to balance and adjust their position leads to crawling, walking, running and jumping.

HAND–EYE COORDINATION ... New-borns have a grasp reflex, whereby they automatically grip objects placed in the hands. When this fades, they learn to pick up objects at will. First, a baby follows an object with their eyes. To reach out, curl their hands around it and pick it up, they need to be able to control and coordinate their movement with what they see. This is known as hand–eye coordination. Handling objects refines their fine motor skills. As their coordination improves, they will form a pincer grip between the thumb and fingers, which is essential for skills such as tooth-brushing or catching a ball.

CROSSING THE "MIDLINE" ... When babies follow a moving object across their field of vision or reach across with the right hand to something on their left side, they cross their midline – an imaginary line down your baby's middle separating the right and left sides of the body. Crossing this line coordinates both sides of the brain, which helps your baby to use opposite sides of the body at the same time, aiding skills such as crawling, and eventually helping to coordinate eye movements to follow words across a page.

Awareness

SPACE AND DISTANCE ... Playing with everyday objects helps your baby to develop spatial awareness – a sense of where their body is in space and in relation to objects around them. When reaching for an object, your baby also has to judge distance and think about how far to move to reach their goal – a skill needed for maths later on.

BODY AWARENESS ... As coordination and movements are refined, your baby develops something known as proprioception – the sense of knowing where different parts of the body are – which enables your baby to carry out actions, such as picking up a cup and drinking from it, without needing to stop, look and think.

RIGHT OR LEFT? ... As your baby explores objects, they may use either hand before developing a preference for one hand or the other.

Understanding

OBJECT PERMANENCE ... Playing peekaboo with objects such as scarves, or putting an object in the bag and taking it out again, teaches your baby that when people or objects are hidden, they are still there. This understanding, known as object permanence, usually develops in the first year. You'll recognise this developmental stage when they look for a covered-up object or one that has rolled away.

MANAGING EMOTIONS ... Playing with objects helps your baby to persevere and build resilience, for example, by having another go at building up blocks. Your baby learns about reactions and emotions from observing your face, tone of voice and gestures.

CAUSE AND EFFECT ... During exploration, your baby sees how actions have consequences – cause and effect – so a shaker makes a noise when it's moved, or a cup empties if tipped.

Maths

EARLY MATHS ... Maths is about so much more than numbers and counting. It is through investigating objects that your baby begins to understand ideas such as size, shape, weight, volume and quantity. Your baby also starts to discover the various properties of objects, for example, a ball will roll away but a sock won't.

FIRST SEQUENCES ... Playing "What's in the Bag?" regularly helps your baby begin to anticipate what is coming next. As well as being fun, this also means your baby starts to recognise the sequence of events and develop a sense of order, a basic concept that forms the foundation for learning about numbers and counting.

Drawing and writing

FIRST MARKS ... Investigating objects and encouraging messy play, for example splodging paint on paper, gives your baby lots of opportunities to start making their first marks. As your baby engages in spontaneous mark making, they gradually acquire the strength, fine motor skills and coordination needed to hold and direct a crayon or pencil.

LEARNING ABOUT MEANING ... When you recognise and value these early marks, you help your baby understand that their actions created the marks and, eventually, that their marks have a meaning. Although it will be a while before your baby forms real letters or connects sounds with words, these early marks are the first step towards the process of drawing and writing.

Communication

BODY LANGUAGE ... Body language is your baby's very first language. As you watch your baby play, notice how they use their eyes to show interest in something, glancing between you and the object in a meaningful way. You can show your mutual interest by following the direction of your baby's gaze.

BUILDING VOCABULARY ... Naming and describing objects helps your baby to form an image of it in their mind and to link the word to the object. Your baby is developing their memory and building up a bank of words. You will see this recognition in action when your baby starts to use objects in appropriate ways during play, such as trying to put a sock on their foot.

Research has found that immersing babies and young children in language, even ideas and words that are beyond their understanding, helps to develop a wide vocabulary, which is linked to complex thinking and is the foundation for doing well in every subject at school.

FIRST SOUNDS ... Babies often babble contentedly to themselves while they are playing, exercising their mouth muscles as they practise the sounds needed for speech development. Your baby might also want to "talk" to you. You can have a wonderful chat without using real words at all. When your baby looks at you with an inviting twinkle in their eye and a tentative sound, repeat the sound then leave a gap for their response. This simple interaction helps your baby understand the turn-taking patterns in real conversations.

POSITIVE INTERACTIONS ... You may find that your baby is particularly responsive if you speak in the gentle, sing–song voice known as "parentese". These first conversations teach your baby about socializing and help them to develop the social skills they will need later on. Your baby will break eye contact and turn away when they need a rest so watch out for this cue.

Discover

What's in the bag

Placing an object in a bag for your baby to find encourages exploration. Staying close by, giving quiet attention and being ready to help if needed, will help your baby feel safe and secure and happy to discover their wonderful new world.

Each time you open the bag...

1 **ANTICIPATE** ... Express interest about what's in the bag and convey this sense of excitement to help your baby anticipate what is coming next.

2 **EXPLORE** ... Encourage your baby to feel the object inside the bag before opening it. Try to guess shapes and sizes to help your baby think about these different properties.

3 **LISTEN** ... Before opening the bag together, help your baby investigate whether the object makes a sound. Does it rustle, rattle or jingle?

4 **DISCOVER** ... Help your baby to open the bag and discover what's inside. Your baby is learning how curiosity and investigation can lead to the reward of discovery.

Object

1

BALL

A ball opens up a world of activity for your baby and ball play is a great way to improve hand–eye coordination.

 YOUNGER BABY ... Your young baby may not yet have the coordination needed to play with a ball but may follow it with their eyes as you roll it around.

 OLDER BABY ... Your on-the-move baby is ready to set off after their ball. Try rolling the ball towards your baby – eventually it may be rolled back.

 TODDLER ... Ball play really starts to open up now. Your little one may manage a first wonky throw or attempt a kick – even if the aim isn't quite there!

...YOU COULD ALSO USE

scrunched-up   a rolled-   an orange
tissue paper   up sock

 # Explore

Once your baby has discovered the ball, here are a few ideas to help you both have fun and learn with it. Make sure the ball is clean and safe to play with.

ROLLING AROUND

Watching a ball rolling can fascinate your baby as it opens up the possibility that circular shapes can move seemingly on their own! Try rolling the ball backwards and forwards at different speeds. Is it moving quickly or slowly? Hearing these words used in context will help to build your baby's vocabulary and understanding.

BUILDING COORDINATION

Watching the ball move from side to side will help to build connections between the two hemispheres of your baby's brain. This in turn helps your baby to coordinate actions and thought processes that require both sides of the brain to work together, such as holding a cup with two hands or crawling.

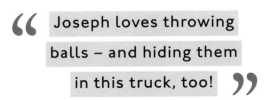

" Joseph loves throwing balls – and hiding them in this truck, too! "

Joseph's mum, Helen

Explore more...

BOLD DESIGNS

Is your baby's ball a bold colour or does it have eye-catching patterns? Mention colours and point out designs. In these early months, your baby is drawn to clear black and white lines, geometrical patterns and primary colours. In time, as their colour vision develops, your baby will spot more subtle shades.

IN THE HAND

As your baby's coordination improves, they will happily grasp a ball with both hands. A ball doesn't have edges or fiddly parts, which makes it easier for babies to hold before they have gained control over the small muscles in their hands that is needed to handle trickier objects.

SENSORY EXPLORATION

Once in your baby's grip, a ball is likely to head straight to their mouth where it can be explored with their sensitive gums. They will discover if it is knobbly, smooth, hard or soft and squidgy. Try describing these textures as your baby handles the ball.

REACHING OUT

Ball play encourages older babies and toddlers to move around, building strength and control. As babies reach out for a ball, they are developing the stability and balance that they need to coordinate their actions.

More Activities

Model turn-taking with your older baby. Roll the ball to your baby, saying **"MY TURN"**. If your baby manages to return it, say **"YOUR TURN"** and applaud your baby's efforts.

Practise **THROWING** the ball with your toddler. Model a throw first then hand the ball to your toddler to have a try.

Song time

Children love to bounce balls, or to watch you bouncing one. Five Little Monkeys ties in perfectly with ball play, reinforcing your baby's understanding of how balls move as well as introducing numbers and counting.

MOVEMENT, NUMBERS AND ORDER

Keep a steady "bouncing" rhythm while you sing or say this rhyme, bouncing your baby up and down in time with the song, or holding your toddler's hands while they jump. These big movements develop spatial awareness as your baby gains a sense of the space that their body takes up while moving. Rhymes with numbers are also a great way to help your baby learn about counting and that numbers have a set order, whether counting up or down.

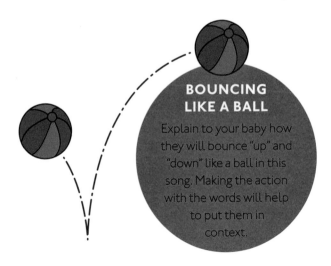

BOUNCING LIKE A BALL

Explain to your baby how they will bounce "up" and "down" like a ball in this song. Making the action with the words will help to put them in context.

Five Little Monkeys

Five little monkeys jumping on the bed.
One fell down and bumped his head.
Mama called the doctor, and the doctor said,
"No more monkeys jumping on the bed!"

Four little monkeys jumping on the bed.
One fell down and bumped his head.
Mama called the doctor, and the doctor said,
"No more monkeys jumping on the bed!"

Three little monkeys jumping on the bed.
One fell down and bumped his head.
Mama called the doctor, and the doctor said,
"No more monkeys jumping on the bed!"

Two little monkeys jumping on the bed.
One fell down and bumped his head.
Mama called the doctor, and the doctor said,
"No more monkeys jumping on the bed!"

One little monkey jumping on the bed.
He fell down and bumped his head.
Mama called the doctor, and the doctor said,
"No more monkeys jumping on the bed!"

No more monkeys jumping on the bed.
None fell down and bumped their head,
Papa called the doctor, and the doctor said,
"Put those monkeys straight to bed!"

CARDBOARD BOX

From construction challenges to pretend play, an empty cardboard box is full of opportunities for your inquisitive baby.

 YOUNGER BABY ... Explore the box together and let your curious baby see the anticipation on your face. What could be inside?

 OLDER BABY ... A baby-sized box can be the ultimate toy for your older baby. Share your baby's delight when you sit them inside and pull them along.

 TODDLER ... Watch out box! Your toddler is likely to be over the moon with this indoor obstacle course and may happily squash the box during their exploits.

...YOU COULD ALSO USE

building blocks   a plastic tub   an eggbox

 # Explore

There are plenty of ways for your baby to get stuck in and enjoy playing with a simple cardboard box. Do supervise play and look out for sharp edges or staples.

EXPLORING SHAPES AND SIZES

The humble cardboard box is a great way to help your baby learn some basic maths concepts. Is your baby's box big or small? If you have more than one box, is one bigger? Talk about shapes, too. Is the box square, long and rectangular, or does it have cut-out circles? As your baby plays, they will explore these properties, sowing the seeds of understanding about sizes and shape.

IN AND OUT

Open the box and pop an object inside to show how smaller objects can fit inside larger ones. Your older baby might enjoy taking the object out and putting it back in, again and again. Repeating tasks cements ideas in your baby's brain. Use positional language such as "in" and "out" to link these actions to words. Show, too, how things can be on top of the box, under it or even go through it.

WHAT'S INSIDE?

A box offers the opportunity for anticipation and discovery. Extend the "in and out" theme with a fun game of hide-and-seek. This will help your baby to understand that objects still exist even when they can't see them. This concept, known as "object permanence", usually develops during the first year of life.

Explore more...

EARLY RHYTHMS

The temptation to bang on a box may be hard for your baby to resist. Offer a wooden spoon and see how your baby is drawn to making a noise – an early attempt at making music! Eventually your baby will learn how sounds can have rhythm, introducing them to song, rhymes and movement and echoing the rhythms of everyday speech.

PATTERNS AND PICTURES

Point out pictures or patterns. Seeing objects depicted in print and hearing the word spoken aloud helps your baby understand that things can be represented in more than one way. A flower might be a real one that can be smelled and touched, it might be a picture or it might be made of paper, but it still has the same name.

OPEN AND SHUT

Your baby might like to open and shut the lid. Watch and see if you can help by holding the box steady. It takes practise to master these complex movements, so this is a great way to help your baby develop hand–eye coordination.

More Activities

Make an **OBSTACLE** course for toddlers. Open out the box for your baby to crawl through.

Stack up different-sized boxes to make a **WOBBLY** tower – ready to be knocked over.

Pretend the box is a **BOAT**, train, bus or house. Draw windows, doors, sails or **WHEELS**.

Song time

The Wheels on the Bus is a great way to practise different movements and to help your baby connect words with actions. You could add to the fun by turning your cardboard box into a bus!

REPEAT AND LEARN

Sing this popular nursery rhyme at a steady pace to create the feeling that you are trundling along on a bus. The simple rhythm and repetition of words will help your baby to link the actions with the words. Leave a gap before you say the final word of a phrase – you might find your baby says it for you! You could also make up your own words based on what you see on the bus. Try beeping the horn on their tummy for an extra giggle.

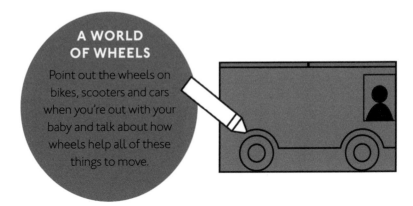

A WORLD OF WHEELS

Point out the wheels on bikes, scooters and cars when you're out with your baby and talk about how wheels help all of these things to move.

The Wheels on the Bus

The wheels on the bus go round and round,
Round and round, round and round.
The wheels on the bus go round and round,
All day long.

The wipers on the bus go swish, swish, swish,
Swish, swish, swish, swish, swish, swish.
The wipers on the bus go swish, swish, swish,
All day long.

The horn on the bus goes beep, beep, beep,
Beep, beep, beep, beep, beep, beep.
The horn on the bus goes beep, beep, beep,
All day long.

The people on the bus go up and down,
Up and down, up and down.
The people on the bus go up and down,
All day long.

STICK

Children love picking up sticks! This simple object grabs their interest and is a great way to start exploring the natural world.

 YOUNGER BABY ... Show your baby the stick, perhaps moving it gently backwards and forwards. Your baby may try to reach out and grab it when it's close enough.

 OLDER BABY ... Your older baby can hold a stick with confidence now and will love waving it around and banging it loudly!

 TODDLER ... Sticks have endless uses for your toddler – a magic wand, a tool to trace patterns in the sand or just something to add to a collection of objects.

...YOU COULD ALSO USE

a wooden spoon   a chunky wooden paintbrush   a toothbrush

Explore

Use some of these ideas to help your baby explore and play with their stick. Check that the stick doesn't go into their mouth or is thrown dangerously around.

NEW TEXTURES AND SHAPES

A stick introduces your baby to interesting new textures, shapes and surfaces. Is your baby's stick knobbly? Does it have a smooth surface, or a slightly rough, uneven one? Is it chunky or thin, long or short? Your baby will store all of this information, which helps to build vocabulary and understanding when you share these words.

SENSORY EXPLORATION

This may be one object you don't want to end up in your baby's mouth, but there's plenty of other sensory stimulation your baby can gather from sticks. As well as touching the stick, listening to the noise it makes when it bangs something and looking at its natural patterns and grains, your baby can also enjoy its woody smell, an exciting discovery for your little one.

" **Isaac explores everything individually, feeling for textures and seeing how it tastes!** "

Isaac's mum, Kerry

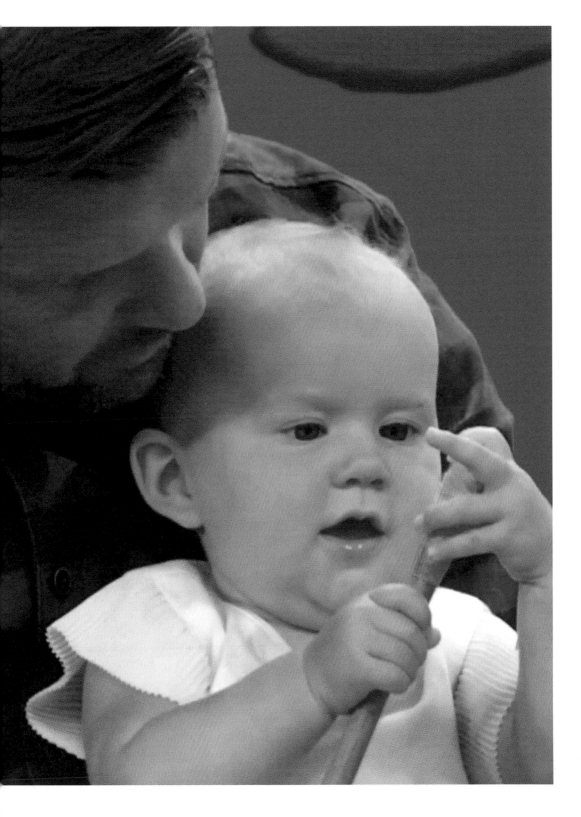

Explore more…

HOLDING TIGHT

Picking up a stick can be a challenge for babies and chunky sticks may be easier to hold. Your older baby is busy developing hand—eye coordination and will watch their hand as it travels towards the stick and their fingers curl around it. Eventually, your baby will be able to judge the distance without tracking their hand.

MAKING A NOISE

Sticks are perfect for banging and making a noise, whether it's hitting two sticks together, or using a stick as a drumstick to bang on another object. As your baby masters this feat of hand—eye coordination, they are also learning how to be in control of making a noise and, with practise, how to make noises louder or softer.

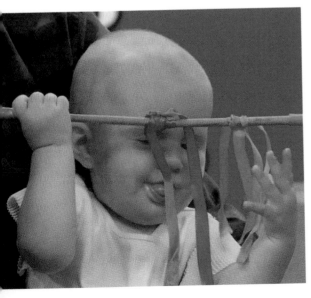

MOVING ABOUT

Your baby may want to wave the stick around. These big movements help your baby strengthen their muscles, gain control over their limbs and, once sitting, manage to balance. All of these movements help them to gain an understanding of where their body is in relation to the space around them.

GET CREATIVE

Try attaching bright ribbons to the stick to make a magic wand. Watch your baby carefully. When they look at the stick, share their interest and look at it, too. If they smile, blink or coo, copy or respond to their reaction. This shared focus will encourage your baby's curiosity.

More Activities

Get out into the **GARDEN** or park and rake up **LEAVES** with the stick.

Show your baby how a stick can draw **SWIRLY** patterns in the sandpit.

 Song time

The classic nursery rhyme, One, Two, Buckle My Shoe uses the popular appeal of sticks to help babies and children learn about numbers and counting. This is a fun way to introduce your baby to some early maths!

COUNT AND SING

Use a marching rhythm and sing-song voice to recite this song. Try saying the numbers clearly and at a slightly slower pace than the rest of the line. This will help familiarise your baby with the names of numbers, such as "one" and "two". Knowing the names for numbers will be a great help with their grasp and understanding of early maths later on.

BEAT A RHYTHM

Have fun gathering sticks in the park. You could use them to beat the rhythm as you sing this song.

One, Two, Buckle My Shoe

One, two, buckle my shoe,
Three, four, knock at the door,
Five, six, pick up sticks,
Seven, eight, lay them straight,
Nine, ten, let's start again.

One, two, buckle my shoe,
Three, four, knock at the door,
Five, six, pick up sticks,
Seven, eight, lay them straight,
Nine, ten, let's start again.

One, two, buckle my shoe,
Three, four, knock at the door,
Five, six, pick up sticks,
Seven, eight, lay them straight,
Nine, ten, let's start again.

PAPER

Paper introduces your baby to the world of mark making and opens up exciting creative possibilities.

 YOUNGER BABY ... Soft tissue paper is perfect for your younger baby. It can be easily scrunched up and is safe to handle and explore.

 OLDER BABY ... Increasingly observant, your older baby may be delighted to discover that a piece of paper can magically float downwards if dropped from up high.

 TODDLER ... Give your toddler a chunky crayon as well as the paper and let them scribble away. Celebrate these first drawings!

...YOU COULD ALSO USE

a leaf   a cardboard   a scarf
           panel from
           a box

 # Explore

Once you've helped your baby shake the bag to tip out the paper, the suggestions here can help you both explore its creative potential. Avoid paper with hard edges.

WATCH IT FLY!

Your baby may love watching a piece of paper float down to the ground when dropped from a height. Chat about what you can see and try using interesting words such as "waft" and "swoop". The more words your baby hears, the more they will learn.

MAKING A MARK

Older babies may enjoy making marks in lots of different ways, including on paper. Try giving them a chunky crayon or some paint to experiment with. If you feel like getting messy, you could help your baby make hand- or footprints, or just let them explore the paint or crayon and paper in their own way. Celebrate their efforts – your interest will help them understand that marks can have meaning. This is the start of learning to read and write.

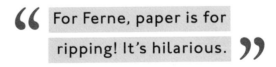

" For Ferne, paper is for ripping! It's hilarious. "

Ferne's mum, Peta

Explore more...

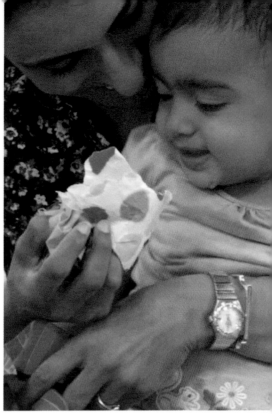

SCRUNCH IT UP

Perhaps your baby will explore the paper by scrunching it up. This simple action stimulates your baby's senses as they see and feel how the paper changes appearance and texture and hear the crunchy sounds. This also helps to strengthen and coordinate the muscles in your baby's arms, hands and fingers. Your baby might be intrigued by watching you scrunch the paper, too and may be keen to explore!

EXPLORING COLOURS

Brightly coloured paper or an array of different coloured paper will catch your baby's eye. Bold primary colours are the ones your baby recognises first, before picking out more subtle shades. This game is a great opportunity to share the names of colours with your baby.

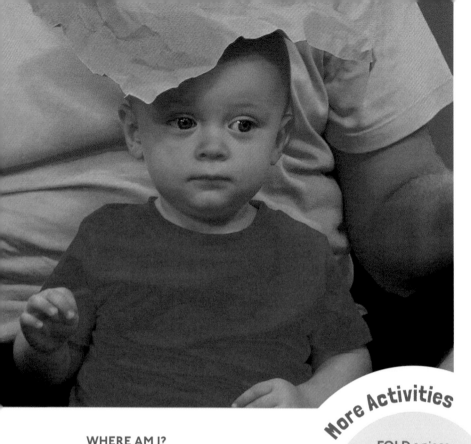

WHERE AM I?

A piece of paper on your baby's head could be a funny hat or a blanket to hide under; or put the paper in front of your face and play peekaboo. Watch your baby's expression as they learn to anticipate your appearance each time. You're helping your baby to understand the concept of object permanence – that when something is hidden it still exists.

More Activities

FOLD a piece of paper up into different **SHAPES** to look at with your baby and introduce them to the idea that something can be transformed.

Wrap a small toy in paper for your baby to **FIND** so they learn how things can be hidden inside something.

 # Song time

Colours are an important part of your baby's world, bringing it to life and helping them identify different objects. If you don't have different-coloured paper for this song, you could look at colours in a magazine.

CELEBRATING COLOUR

Say the rainbow rhyme in a gentle sing-song voice or sing it to a familiar tune. Each time you say a colour draw out the word so your baby catches this emphasis. You could let your baby hold a piece of scrunched-up paper as you sing the verses, helping them practise gaining control over the small muscles in their hand.

NEW COLOURS OF THE RAINBOW

You could try adding some unusual colours into the song, such as scarlet or mauve. Every new word builds your baby's vocabulary.

Colours of the Rainbow

Yellow paper, yellow paper,
scrunched up small, in a ball,

Colours of the rainbow, colours of the rainbow,
We love them all, we love them all.

Red paper, red paper,
scrunched up small, in a ball,

Colours of the rainbow, colours of the rainbow,
We love them all, we love them all.

Blue paper, blue paper,
scrunched up small, in a ball,

Colours of the rainbow, colours of the rainbow,
We love them all, we love them all.

Purple paper, purple paper,
scrunched up small, in a ball,

Colours of the rainbow, colours of the rainbow,
We love them all, we love them all.

PURE BRISTLES

PAINTBRUSH

A paintbrush encourages creativity and exploration. Soon, your baby may be making their first marks!

 YOUNGER BABY ... Bristles are an intriguing sensation for your baby and present a new challenge for them to grasp then manage to hold.

 OLDER BABY ... Your baby is busy fine-tuning hand movements and gaining control of their limbs. Picking up a brush and guiding it to paper uses both of these skills.

 TODDLER ... Things could get messy now. Armed with a brush and paint, your toddler may get stuck in and happily splodge and splatter away!

...YOU COULD ALSO USE

a stick   a toothbrush   a wooden spoon

Explore

Look in the bag to find the paintbrush. You could put out some child-friendly paint and paper, too. Use a new or clean brush that has had only child-friendly, non-toxic paint on it.

TICKLE ME
Your baby might like to be tickled gently on their hands or feet with a soft brush. Watch to see how they react. You might need to reassure them about this strange new bristly sensation, or they might love it and want you to play the game again and again.

EXPLORING COLOURS
If you wish, put out some bright, child-friendly paint and a piece of paper and let your baby dab the brush in and make a colourful splodge. Show delight at your baby's creation! Putting brush to paper also involves your baby judging the distance to see how far they need to reach.

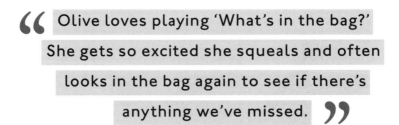

" Olive loves playing 'What's in the bag?' She gets so excited she squeals and often looks in the bag again to see if there's anything we've missed. "

Olive's dad, Reece

Explore more...

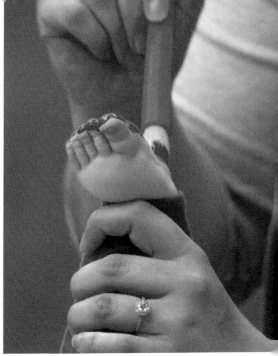

ALL SORTS OF BRUSHES

Give your baby different types of brushes to explore, such as a soft bath brush or a wall brush, as well as a traditional small paintbrush so your baby can experience bristles and brushes in a variety of shapes and sizes. Watch carefully to see what your baby shows a particular interest in, then share their focus and show that you are interested, too.

FIRST MARKS

Your baby's first marks are an important step, signalling the start of their journey to drawing and writing. Noticing these marks is key as your recognition will encourage your baby to try again. If you are happy to get messy, you could let your baby explore making marks with their hands or feet rather than with the brushes. Look at their hand- or footprint together with delight.

MESSY PLAY

Being creative with a paintbrush can be a messy business, but letting your baby get stuck in has lots of benefits. As well as exploring textures and learning to control the small muscles in the hand to hold and move the brush, your baby also builds confidence and self-esteem and learns about creativity.

REACHING ACROSS

Painting encourages your baby to twist and turn their body. When your baby reaches from left to right or vice versa, they cross the "midline" of their body, which helps to connect the two halves of the brain and coordinate movement on both sides of the body.

More Activities

Gather brushes of various **SIZES** and see all the different effects that your baby can make.

Try simply wetting the paintbrush and let your baby have fun making **WATER MARKS** on a piece of coloured paper or on some paving stones.

 Song time

In the delightful Finger Family song, you could use your fingers as props. Paint your fingertips then wiggle each one in time with the verses, replacing the finger names with people or relationships important to you.

PLEASED TO MEET YOU

Make up your own tune or say the words to the song in a sing-song voice, making your voice a little higher as you ask where each finger is and lower with each greeting. Shake your baby's hand as you say "How do you do?" to help your baby start to understand social interactions and relationships. Your baby will also warm to the family theme of this song, which signals inclusion and love.

FUNNY FINGERS

Have even more fun with your painted fingertips – give each finger its own voice and make your baby chuckle by holding a silly pretend conversation.

Finger Family

Daddy finger, Daddy finger, where are you?
Here I am, here I am, how do you do?

Mummy finger, Mummy finger, where are you?
Here I am, here I am, how do you do?

Brother finger, brother finger, where are you?
Here I am, here I am, how do you do?

Sister finger, sister finger, where are you?
Here I am, here I am, how do you do?

Baby finger, baby finger, where are you?
Here I am, here I am, how do you do?

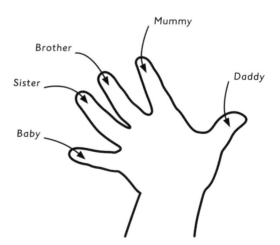

SOFT TOY

Your baby may feel an instant rapport with their soft toy! Have fun engaging them in some pretend play.

 YOUNGER BABY ... Your baby may be fascinated with the toy's face and might hug the toy, forming a bond and enjoying its soft, soothing texture.

 OLDER BABY ... Soft toys come into their own now, offering reassurance if your baby becomes upset when away from you.

 TODDLER ... A soft toy may be a fairly constant companion, taking on near-human attributes as it continues to offer comfort to your toddler.

...YOU COULD ALSO USE

a sock puppet   **a rubber duck**   **a doll**

 # Explore

Watch your baby's reaction as they discover a soft toy in the bag, then let them enjoy a cuddle if they wish. Here are some ideas to help your baby's play. Watch out for any small parts that would be a choking hazard.

WHICH ANIMAL AM I?

Soft toys are a great way for your baby to learn about the world of animals. Talk about the soft toy to your baby – which animal is it, does it have stripes or spots and what noises does it make? Introduce noises that other animals make, too, so your baby learns how each animal has its own identity. Watch how your baby reacts to these sounds. Are they smiling, or a little apprehensive? Let your baby see your mouth as you make the sounds. Your baby will be encouraged to copy you, learning to coordinate the tiny muscles in their mouth and eventually make their own first animal noises. Copying you is one of your baby's first steps on the way to learning to talk.

> **Dhilan loves cuddling his toys and saying goodnight to each of them at bedtime.**

Dhilan's dad, Andrew

Explore more...

CUDDLE UP

When your baby cuddles a soft toy, as well as simply enjoying the sensation, they learn some important things, such as how to express feelings, show empathy (eventually) and enjoy socializing. Give the soft toy a big cuddle, too, so your baby can mimic your behaviour and learn about relationships and positive interactions.

LET'S PRETEND

Your older baby is starting to enjoy pretend play. Help your baby explore this exciting new aspect of play – pretend to feed their soft toy, talk to it, and rock it to sleep. These interactions with their toy will help to develop your baby's social skills. Make up fun stories, too: "Where is Mr Lion off to in the jungle today?", "Hoppity hop, here's Miss Frog!".

FURRY FUN

Soft furry toys are the ultimate in comfort and their texture can evoke strong feelings in your baby. As your baby nestles in, they discover that the sensation creates happy, secure feelings, while you observe the calming effect of the soft toy.

WHAT'S NEXT?

Soft toy play can be full of fun. If your baby is in the mood, hold the toy away from them so they can focus on it then bring it to them for a kiss or cuddle. They might be surprised, but may be happy to play again, next time anticipating what is coming!

More Activities

Host a teddy's **TEA PARTY** in the garden for your toddler, complete with paper cups and plates.

Point to the parts of a soft toy's face, saying "Where is the **NOSE**?", "Here are the **EARS!**", to help your baby learn the names for these different features.

Help your baby arrange their soft toys from **SMALLEST** to **BIGGEST** so they start to grasp maths ideas such as size.

Song time

Animals are fun for babies and children and Old MacDonald Had a Farm really captures this feeling with its lively beat and entertaining animal sounds. Bring the farmyard to your baby as you enjoy this song together.

NOISY AND FUN

Keep the tempo quick and upbeat as you run through the verses. Each time you get to an animal, make the noise as convincingly as you can so your baby learns that animals can be identified through the sounds they make as well as by how they look. Have fun swapping in some exotic animals – try a snake or a lion! The repetitive verses will help your baby absorb and learn words and start to get used to the ideas of order and sequence.

QUACK

QUACK QUACK

QUACK

PUT IT INTO WORDS

As well as acting out animal noises, point out the words for the noises whenever you see these in books and print.

Old MacDonald Had a Farm

Old Macdonald had a farm, E-I-E-I-O.
And on his farm he had a cow, E-I-E-I-O.
With a "moo moo" here and a "moo moo" there,
Here a "moo", there a "moo",
Everywhere a "moo moo".
Old Macdonald had a farm, E-I-E-I-O.

Old Macdonald had a farm, E-I-E-I-O.
And on his farm he had a pig, E-I-E-I-O.
With a (snort) here and a (snort) there,
Here a (snort), there a (snort),
Everywhere a (snort-snort).
Old Macdonald had a farm, E-I-E-I-O.

Old Macdonald had a farm, E-I-E-I-O.
And on his farm he had a horse, E-I-E-I-O.
With a "neigh, neigh" here and a "neigh, neigh" there,
Here a "neigh", there a "neigh",
Everywhere a "neigh, neigh".
Old Macdonald had a farm, E-I-E-I-O.

Old Macdonald had a farm, E-I-E-I-O.
And on his farm he had a duck, E-I-E-I-O.
With a "quack, quack" here and a "quack, quack" there,
Here a "quack", there a "quack",
Everywhere a "quack, quack".
Old Macdonald had a farm, E-I-E-I-O.

SOCK

A sock may not seem like an obvious play object but can be fun, prompting pretend play and helping learning in lots of ways.

 YOUNGER BABY ... A sock is likely to find its way straight to your baby's mouth. Satisfyingly soft and easy to hold, your baby will perfect their sucking skills!

 OLDER BABY ... Your increasingly observant baby may be ready to start noticing things such as a sock's colour, size or a pattern when you point these out.

 TODDLER ... Curious and in to everything, your toddler is likely to rummage around to see if anything is hidden inside their sock!

...YOU COULD ALSO USE

gloves   a hat   a scarf

 # Explore

Shake the bag with your baby to tip the sock, or selection of socks, out. Share your enthusiasm, using the ideas here to help your baby explore and have fun.

PUPPET PLAY

Entertain your baby with some puppet play. Pop your hand into the sock to transform it into something else, such as a friendly snake. Make a wavy action and give the snake a silly voice then tell a story about the snake. This fun, positive interaction opens up the possibility of storytelling.

FIRST "CONVERSATIONS"

Have an animated chat with the sock puppet. Ask it a question then pause before getting the puppet to answer in a different voice. Get the puppet to ask your baby a question, pausing again to let them respond – with a smile, a giggle, a movement or perhaps just a blink. Acknowledge your baby's response. This back-and-forth interaction models the art of turn-taking in conversations and shows your baby how words and actions can convey meaning.

 Ferne knows exactly where her socks go and tries to put them on her feet herself.

Ferne's mum, Peta

Explore more...

HIDE-AND-SEEK

Pop an object in the sock and play a game of hide-and-seek. As well as helping your baby realise that an object still exists when it can't be seen and to understand concepts such as "in and out", you are also helping your baby build a visual memory bank as an image of the hidden object will be retained in their mind.

SORT IT OUT

Socks are made for sorting. Jumble up some pairs then play spot the difference with your baby. Say why some socks are different then find their matching pair. Get your older baby or toddler to help you sort the socks and count out the pairs. This is a perfect way to introduce early maths ideas into your baby's playtime.

A WORLD OF SHAPES

Look at shapes and patterns on the socks. Are there stars, circles, hearts or diamonds? Or are there stripes or zigzags? Name these shapes and patterns to help your baby absorb all of this information and develop both language and early maths skills. Point out similar shapes elsewhere to reinforce the learning.

More Activities

Roll up a sock and **THROW** it in the air. Let your older baby or toddler join in or direct the play.

Play the "stinky sock" game. Put the sock on your baby's foot. Take a big sniff, then say **"PHEWEE!"** and pretend to faint, knocked out by the smell! Watch your baby dissolve in giggles.

 # Song time

Socks naturally make us think about our feet, so Head, Shoulders, Knees and Toes is the perfect way to wind up sock play with your baby – and help them to think about other parts of their body as well.

HEAD TO TOE

Touch the parts of your baby's body as you name each one in the song, or sit opposite your older baby or toddler so they can copy your actions. This tuneful song can be repeated two or three times, each time stepping up the pace a little so that the actions are faster. As well as making this entertaining, it also helps your older baby or toddler focus hard on coordinating their actions in time with the song – applaud whatever your baby manages to do.

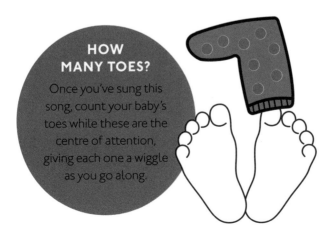

HOW MANY TOES?

Once you've sung this song, count your baby's toes while these are the centre of attention, giving each one a wiggle as you go along.

Head, Shoulders, Knees and Toes

Head, shoulders,
knees and toes,
knees and toes.

Head, shoulders,
knees and toes,
knees and toes.

And eyes and ears and mouth and nose.

Head, shoulders,
knees and toes,
knees and toes.

Object 8

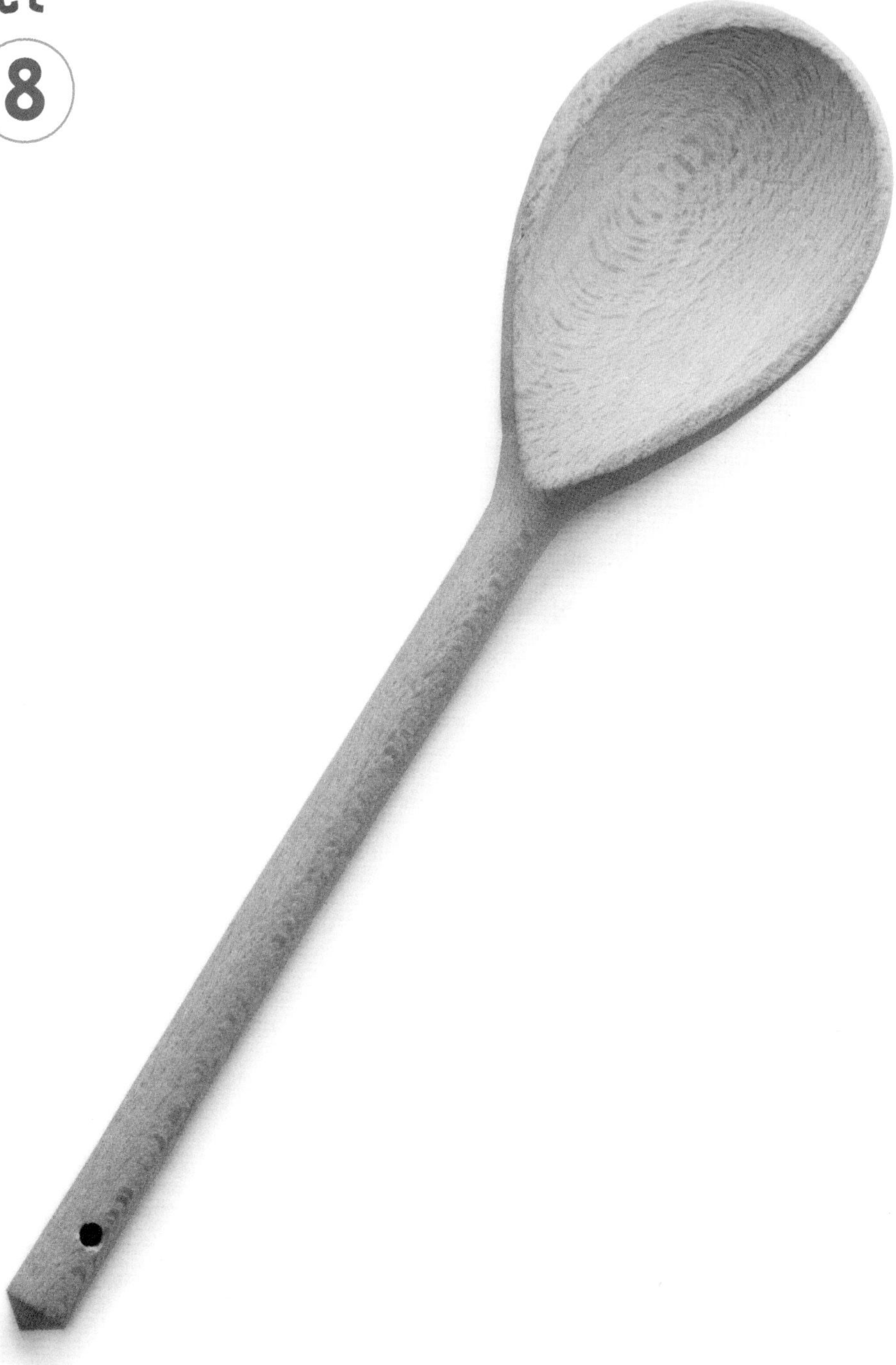

WOODEN SPOON

This everyday utensil, with its natural textures, patterns and intriguing shapes, has plenty of play potential.

 YOUNGER BABY ... A wooden spoon gives your baby plenty of opportunity to explore its interesting shape and texture.

 OLDER BABY ... Learning to coordinate the fingers to pick up a wooden spoon is perfect practise for your baby's emerging hand–eye coordination.

 TODDLER ... Don't stand too close! Your toddler has boundless energy and is likely to wave the spoon back and forth with great enthusiasm.

...YOU COULD ALSO USE

a stick   a paintbrush   a hairbrush

Explore

Once you've pulled the wooden spoon out of the bag together, use the tips here to help your baby explore. Make sure the spoon is clean and without rough edges.

HOLD TIGHT

The long handle of a wooden spoon provides a good surface to grip. Your younger baby may find it quite challenging to coordinate their fingers around the slim handle and may opt to hold on to the cupped end. If your baby hasn't mastered picking up objects yet, try putting it in their hand so that they can use their grasp reflex to hold it tight. Your older baby is rapidly refining their grip and a wooden spoon offers a great opportunity to improve hand–eye coordination and dexterity. Your baby's eyes direct their hand to the spoon, then they focus hard to control their hand muscles and curl their fingers around the handle – actions that will eventually help your baby to master the skills needed to draw and write.

WAVE IT ALL ABOUT

Once your baby has a hold of the spoon, they are likely to wave it around, which helps to build up strength in their arm muscles. Moving the limbs also helps develop spatial awareness as your baby notices the space that they take up while moving.

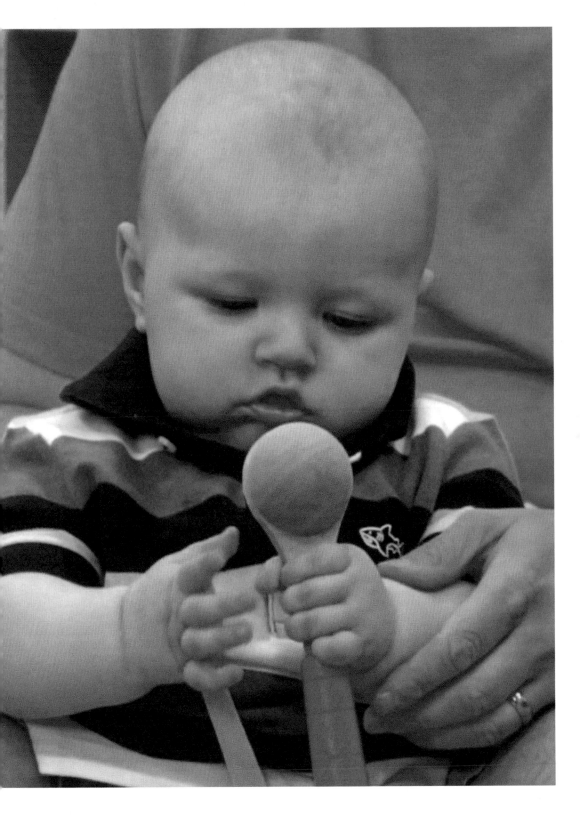

Explore more...

HIT A BEAT

Your baby can make a satisfying noise with a wooden spoon. Let your baby bang two spoons together or put out some pots and pans to make a drum kit to beat a rhythm on. Making a noise in this way encourages self-expression and helps your baby tune in to different beats. Count a simple one, two marching beat to accompany your baby and familiarise them with these key numbers.

LONG AND SHORT

Give your baby different-sized spoons and point out how one is longer and one is shorter. Is one spoon also wider and one narrow and thin? Describing the spoons' properties introduces your baby to these basic mathematical ideas.

ACT IT OUT

Your baby loves to copy you and learns by mimicking your actions. Pretend to stir the spoon in a bowl, then to eat some food from it. Offer your baby a spoonful. Your older baby may try some stirring actions and offer you a mouthful in turn, while your toddler may feed their teddies. These actions teach your baby about turn-taking and also help to develop their hand–eye coordination.

NATURAL PATTERNS

Notice how your baby explores the spoon's patterns and texture. Show your interest with a nod or a smile and say words such as "rough" or "smooth" while your baby touches the spoon.

More Activities

Make a wooden spoon **PUPPET**. Tie a cloth on for a skirt and draw a **HAPPY** face on one side and a **SAD** face on the other so your baby sees these two emotions.

Gather some pans and plastic bowls and enjoy a pretend **COOKING** session together.

🥄 Song time

This curious rhyme introduces some interesting themes and ideas. It is ideal to sing while your baby is exploring the wooden spoon. Encourage your older baby to act out the words as you sing together.

MIME ALONG

Sing this song expressively to convey feelings such as fear and surprise, which may be new concepts to your baby. Mime eating with a spoon as you sing to see if your baby copies your actions with their wooden spoon. Move your fingers in a pitter-patter action to suggest the spider's action and help your baby understand positional words such as "beside" and "along".

**TIME
TO EAT**

Acting out scenarios – such as pretending to eat from a bowl – in time with a song or rhyme can help your baby master these skills in real life.

Little Miss Muffet

Little Miss Muffet sat on a tuffet

Eating her curds and whey,

Along came a spider,

Who sat down beside her

And frightened Miss Muffet away.

Little Miss Muffet sat on a tuffet

Eating her curds and whey,

Along came a spider,

Who sat down beside her

And frightened Miss Muffet away.

BATH TOY

Bath toys open up the exciting possibility of water play. Your baby can discover the joys of filling, pouring, floating and more!

 YOUNGER BABY ... Bath toys can grab your young baby's attention and help to make bathtime one of the favourite parts of the day.

 OLDER BABY ... Your older baby might marvel at how water runs through a cup with holes or a mini watering can and will want to fill these up again and again.

 TODDLER ... Your toddler might love splashing about and is ready to be immersed in some pretend play – try sailing on the high seas!

...YOU COULD ALSO USE

a rubber duck   a sponge   a plastic tub
                               or cup

Explore

Help your baby rummage inside the bag for the bath toy then have fun trying some of the suggestions here together. Supervise your baby at all times during water play.

SPLISH SPLASH

Have a bowl of water ready and encourage your baby to experience the wetness of water by putting their toy in the bowl. Afterwards, say "Let's get dry!" to help your baby recognise these different states. Dip your hands in the water, too, and describe if it's cold or warm. During water play, use descriptive words such as "splash", "splosh" and "plop", making these noises in the water as you say them.

WATCH IT FLOAT

Science concepts fascinate babies. If your baby has a boat, or other floating toy, pop it on top of the water to show floating in action. Find an object that sinks and drop this in the water to show how lighter objects might float and heavier ones can sink. If you don't have water, you could pretend. Try lifting your baby up and down to bob along like the boat.

QUACKETY QUACK

A rubber duck has a lot to offer. You could try singing a song about a duck or even making up a short story. Does the duck make a noise when you squeeze it? See if your baby wants to have a go. Squeezing helps your baby practise their grip and develops strength and control of the small muscles in the hands and fingers, key skills for eating or writing later on.

Explore more...

WATER THE PLANTS

Involving babies and toddlers in everyday tasks is a great way to help them learn. Pretend to water flowers with a mini watering can, or, if you have a garden or window box, let your little one help water the plants. Chat about how the can is heavy when full and light when empty, which introduces early maths ideas such as weight, volume and capacity.

COLOURS, SHAPES AND SIZES

Bath toys come in lots of colours, shapes and sizes. Is your baby filling up the red cup or playing with the long boat or the round duck? Your baby listens constantly, soaking up information. Using descriptive words builds their vocabulary, eventually helping them to talk and to recognise written words.

CAUSE AND EFFECT

Playing with bath toys shows how actions have consequences – cause and effect. This could be the splash that happens when a hand hits water, the plop when something sinks or the noise a toy makes when squeezed.

FILL IT UP

Bath cups with holes for water to run through are captivating. Show your baby how this works and encourage your older baby to have a go to see how things can be full then empty. Your baby is also learning about types of movement. Describe how water flows smoothly, or can be choppy when splashed.

More Activities

Use empty, cleaned yogurt pots in the bath for your baby to fill up and **POUR** from. You could make some holes in the bottom for water to stream through.

A **SPONGE** is a great way to show your baby how water makes objects heavy then how squeezing it out makes them light.

🚢 Song time

A much-loved nursery rhyme, Row, Row, Row Your Boat is lots of fun to sing both in and out of the bath. You and your baby can have fun acting out the rowing motions, going faster or slower as you wish.

MOVING TOGETHER

Sing this lively song with your baby on your lap, or, if they can sit well, sit opposite and hold hands as you gently guide your baby back and forth. As well as enjoying plenty of eye-to-eye contact, which is reassuring and comforting, your baby also gets to work on perfecting their balance – supported by you – and builds strength in their limbs as you both move together with the song.

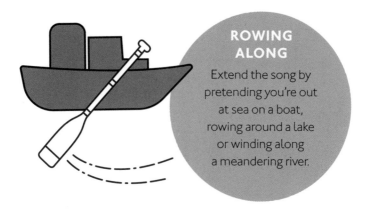

ROWING ALONG

Extend the song by pretending you're out at sea on a boat, rowing around a lake or winding along a meandering river.

Row, Row, Row Your Boat

Row, row, row your boat

Gently down the stream,

Merrily merrily, merrily, merrily,

Life is but a dream.

Row, row, row your boat

Gently down the stream,

Merrily merrily, merrily, merrily,

Life is but a dream.

BUILDING BLOCKS

Blocks not only offer exciting construction challenges, they also introduce your baby to some basic maths.

 YOUNGER BABY ... Managing to grasp a block is challenge enough for your younger baby who will then happily explore the block with their mouth.

 OLDER BABY ... Your baby's control of their limbs is steadily improving and they will have lots of fun knocking down the tower you've carefully built up!

 TODDLER ... Your little one is ready to build! Let your toddler have a go and be ready to step in and help if needed.

...YOU COULD ALSO USE

different-sized
cardboard boxes

plastic
cups

small and large
plastic tubs

 # Explore

Shake the bag to tip out the blocks together. You could have a selection of blocks or just one type. Use the ideas here to help your baby explore and learn.

LOOKING AT SHAPES AND SIZES

As your baby explores the blocks, talk about different shapes and sizes to introduce these early maths ideas. Describe how some shapes have edges and others curves. Name the shapes and talk to your older baby about comparisons such as bigger and smaller. If you have a shape sorter, this is a great way for your baby to learn about shapes as they experiment to find how shapes fit.

NOTICING COLOURS

What colours can you see with your baby? Your baby loves looking at bright colours and is likely to be drawn to these. Name the colours to build vocabulary and help your baby recognise, compare and contrast them. Make associations – for example, "This block is blue, like the sea".

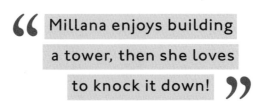

❝ Millana enjoys building a tower, then she loves to knock it down! ❞

Millana's mum, Louise

Explore more...

COUNT THEM UP

Have fun building up a tower of blocks together. You could count the blocks as they stack up so that your baby starts to absorb the words for numbers and also learns that numbers have a set order and sequence. When you count backwards and forwards you'll reinforce these sequences, teaching that the order of numbers is set.

BUILD UP, FALL DOWN

Building up a tower then letting your baby knock it down shows that actions have consequences – cause and effect. Focusing on placing a brick helps older babies and toddlers develop the hand–eye coordination needed to master these complex actions. If the tower topples over, encourage your baby to have another go to build resilience.

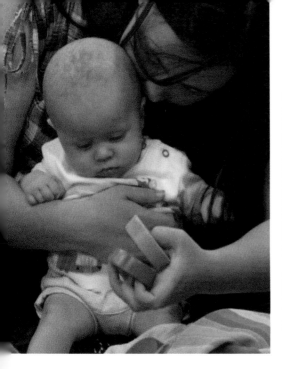

MAKING NOISES

Watch your baby as they explore the blocks. Are they banging them together and making a noise? Try joining in and show how you can make loud or quiet noises and different rhythms. Your interest will help them feel good about themselves.

EXPLORING TEXTURE

Are your baby's blocks hard and smooth, or soft and squishy? Do some textures look as well as feel different? Chat to your baby about how textures can affect us; for example, how soft textures can be soothing when we touch them.

More Activities

Help your baby to sort the blocks by **COLOUR** then by size to explore these groups.

Try building towers in a variety of **SHAPES**. Create a pyramid-shaped tower, or a tower with an **ARCH** and talk to your baby about all the shapes you can spot in the tower.

Play a memory game with your toddler. **HIDE** two or three blocks under a piece of paper then ask how many are there.

Song time

The Grand Old Duke of York is a great nursery rhyme to reinforce the theme of numbers and also develops your baby's conceptual awareness of actions such as up and down and side to side.

A MARCHING BEAT

Sing this marching song to a quick one, two beat. Your baby might enjoy being moved in time with the actions, up and down and side to side, and this will help them connect these positional words with the movements. If your baby can stand, hold both their hands and march together. This will help your baby strengthen their big leg muscles and develop coordination and balance.

MARCHING FINGERS

Try marching up and down a tower of blocks with your fingers while you sing along for a gentler way to enjoy this song.

The Grand Old Duke of York

Oh, the grand old Duke of York,
He had ten thousand men.
He marched them up to the top of the hill,
Then he marched them down again.

And when they were up, they were up.
And when they were down, they were down.
And when they were only halfway up
They were neither up nor down.

Oh, the grand old Duke of York,
He marched low and up high.
He marched his men to the top of the hill,
They could almost touch the sky.

(Chorus)

Oh, the grand old Duke of York,
He marched from side to side.
He marched his men to the top of the hill,
They could see so far and wide.

(Chorus)

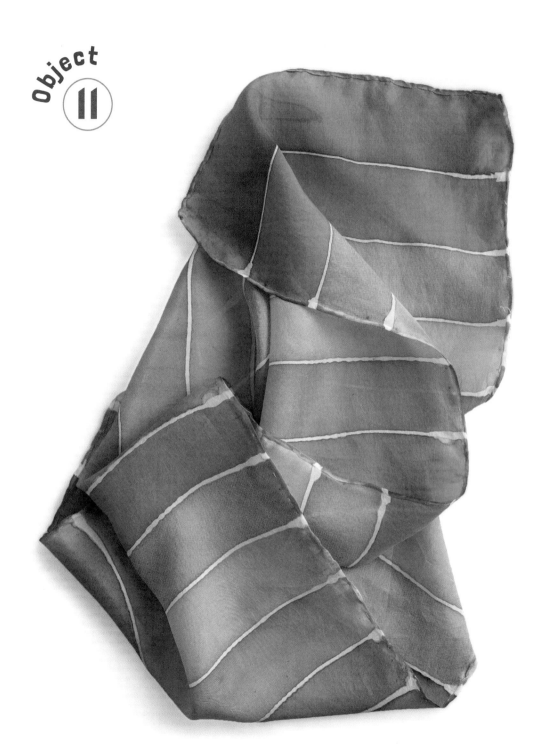

SCARF

As well as feeling lovely, scarves are perfect for discovery games – whether hiding an object, you or your baby!

 YOUNGER BABY ... Playing with a scarf is a sensory feast for your baby, as they experience how it feels, looks and even tastes.

 OLDER BABY ... Your baby might never have enough of peekaboo, and a scarf is the ideal item for this game. Be prepared to "peekaboo" again and again!

 TODDLER ... A scarf can be endless fun for your toddler – used as a kite to run with, a cover to hide under or a colourful piece of clothing to dress up in.

...YOU COULD ALSO USE

paper   **a ribbon**   **a blanket**

 # Explore

Once you've helped your baby pull the scarf out of the bag, unravel it and let your baby explore how it feels, moves and looks – keeping an eye that they don't get in a tangle.

PEEKABOO

Your baby's scarf is perfect for a game of peekaboo – hide your or your baby's face behind the scarf, then take it away and say "peekaboo!". This favourite game appeals across the age groups, meaning different things at different stages. In your baby's first year, peekaboo helps your baby slowly grasp the idea that you are still there even when you can't be seen. By toddlerhood, your little one knows what's coming next and is simply gleeful with anticipation!

HOW DOES IT FEEL?

Scarves are soothing textures for babies – whether soft, woolly, silky or furry. Your baby will love nuzzling into a scarf, conjuring up feelings of warmth and comfort similar to those they experience when enjoying a cuddle with you.

> **Playing peekaboo with a scarf is Joseph's favourite game.**

Joseph's mum, Helen

Explore more...

TICKLY SNAKE

Engage your baby in some amusing pretend play with the scarf. Turn the scarf into a friendly snake, come to tickle your baby. As well as helping your baby think about how play can be extended into pretend worlds, they will also enjoy this positive interaction with you, which in turn builds self-esteem and helps your baby feel secure.

PATTERNS AND COLOURS

Scarves are full of patterns, stripes and colours. Bold stripes, bright colours and clear designs stand out to your baby while their colour vision develops. Point these out to help your baby recognise shapes and colours and learn their names. Finding out about patterns and shapes also familiarises them with these early maths ideas.

WAVING AROUND

Scarves are made for waving.
As your baby or toddler waves
the scarf enthusiastically, they
are exercising the large muscles
in their limbs, learning to
balance, and also developing
spatial awareness – becoming
aware of where their body is
in relation to its surroundings.

HIDE-AND-SEEK

Extend the peekaboo theme
with a game of hide-and-seek.
Hide an object under the scarf
and ask your baby where it is.
This helps develop your baby's
visual memory as they hold
a picture in their mind, and
also encourages your baby to
persevere and find the object.

More Activities

Make a
DEN out of
several scarves for
your baby or toddler
to enjoy. Peek in and
say **"BOO!"**.

Gather
some colourful
scarves and help your
baby **DRESS UP** their
favourite **TEDDIES**
and **DOLLS**, ready
for a special
occasion.

Song time

Have fun singing this scarf song with your baby, which brings in movement, tickling, and the element of surprise – all things your baby might enjoy. Encourage your baby to wave the scarf from side to side as you sing.

FULL OF SURPRISES

Sing or say the words to the scarf song to a rhythmic beat, focusing on the movement and actions – waving scarves high, low and round and round to help your baby connect words and actions. When your baby joins in with these moves, they are learning how to control their limbs and to balance. On "Say hello", dangle the scarf in front of your baby's face, then pull it away to say "Boo!". As this is repeated in each verse, your baby will be ready for the thrill!

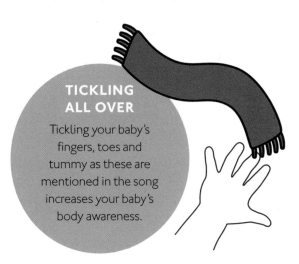

TICKLING ALL OVER

Tickling your baby's fingers, toes and tummy as these are mentioned in the song increases your baby's body awareness.

Scarves are Waving

Scarves are waving,
Scarves are waving.
High and low,
Round they go.

> Tickling your tummy,
> Tickling your tummy.
> Say hell–o – BOO!
> Say hell–o – BOO!

Scarves are waving,
Scarves are waving.
High and low,
Round they go.

> Tickling your fingers,
> Tickling your fingers.
> Say hell–o – BOO!
> Say hell–o – BOO!

Scarves are waving,
Scarves are waving.
High and low,
Round they go.

> Tickling your toes,
> Tickling your toes.
> Say hell–o – BOO!
> Say hell–o – BOO!

CUPS

From stacking up to holding impromptu tea parties, or for simply exploring, cups can be lots of fun for your baby.

 YOUNGER BABY ... A cup has no right or wrong way up for your curious younger baby as they explore it with all their senses.

 OLDER BABY ... Handling a cup is ideal practise for hand–eye coordination as your baby needs to learn to pick it up then focus on guiding it to their mouth.

 TODDLER ... Your active toddler can find all sorts of uses for a cup. Let your toddler direct the play and be ready to join in and enjoy an afternoon tea party!

...YOU COULD ALSO USE

    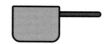

plastic tub   **bowl**   **small pan**

 # Explore

Discover the cup together. Try to have one for you and one for your baby, then model how you pick it up. Here are some ideas to help your baby explore the non-breakable cup.

ON TOP AND BELOW

Make your baby laugh by using the cup as a hat. As well as being hilarious, this introduces positional language such as "on top of", "below" and "under". Marrying words with actions builds brain connections and aids memory. You're also teaching how one thing can represent another, leading to all sorts of fun possibilities!

HAVE SOME TEA!

Babies learn how things work from watching you. With your older baby, try taking a "sip" from your cup and saying "Mmm, delicious!". You might find that your baby copies you and starts to enjoy their own pretend cup of tea. This is a great start in your baby learning how to use a cup to drink from.

> " 'What's in the bag?' works so well for Luther and me. It gives a focus and encourages us to use objects in different ways. "

Luther's mum, Nicole

Explore more...

PERFECTLY STACKED

Watching you stack up cups teaches your baby how one shape fits inside another. Once your baby can sit and has greater hand control, they can have a go. Your baby is learning several things at once here – the properties of shapes as well as how to control actions. Build on this activity – count the cups and name colours to introduce numbers and build your baby's bank of words.

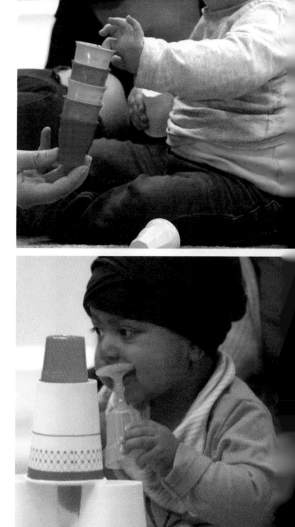

BUILD THEM HIGH

Amaze your baby by demonstrating how cups can be turned upside-down and used to create a tower. Show your younger baby how you can build the cups into a triangle-shaped tower and describe this shape. Your toddler can help you build the cups up and, as with building blocks, will have fun knocking the tower down – then starting again.

POUR IT OUT

Give your baby a bowl of tepid water with the cups and get pouring. Older babies might enjoy filling a cup, emptying it out then repeating this again and again. Repetition builds connections in the brain and strengthens understanding of ideas such as cause and effect and empty and full.

More Activities

Use the base of a cup as a **DRUM** kit and give your baby a wooden spoon to make some music with!

Gather cups and plates and suggest a teddy bear's **PICNIC** for your baby's favourite soft toys.

ALL SORTS

Cups come in lots of different shapes, sizes and materials. Metal cups can have shiny silver surfaces, while egg cups may be made of wood. Describe these and chat about their uses.

🍵 Song time

A classic nursery rhyme, Polly Put the Kettle On is fun to sing with your baby, using their cup as a prop. Your baby might recognise the familiar routine of making a drink and the chance for some pretend play.

ACT IT OUT

Use an expressive voice while you sing and make a happy face as the tea is made, then a sad face when the kettle is taken off again to help your baby recognise these emotions. Repeating the verses gives a sense of order as your baby anticipates what happens next. Swap your baby's name in on one verse and see how they react. They will probably be delighted. Using their name in playful ways helps to develop a sense of identity.

POUR IT CAREFULLY

If you have a plastic teapot, fill this with water and help your older baby practise filling up their cup – a feat of coordination!

Polly Put the Kettle On

Polly put the kettle on,
Polly put the kettle on,
Polly put the kettle on,
We'll all have tea.

Sukey take it off again,
Sukey take it off again,
Sukey take it off again,
They've all gone away.

Polly put the kettle on,
Polly put the kettle on,
Polly put the kettle on,
We'll all have tea.

Sukey take it off again,
Sukey take it off again,
Sukey take it off again,
They've all gone away.

Opportunities...

For exploring, playing and learning ...
There are plenty of ways to weave play into
everyday routines, which in turn helps to
build your baby's confidence, self-esteem
and physical and cognitive skills. Use the
suggestions here to help you build play
into whatever you're doing with your baby.

Getting dressed

EXPLORE TEXTURES ... Try describing what different items of clothing feel like. Is a hat soft and woolly, are the wellingtons firm and smooth or does a jumper have a bumpy pattern?

MAKE A PUPPET ... Make a hand puppet with a sock or glove and have a puppet "conversation" with your baby. Ask a question and watch to see how they respond, perhaps with a look, sound or action. Showing that you are listening helps develop their own listening skills.

ONE, TWO ... These are the first numbers your baby learns so use them whenever you can. Count "one arm through, two arms through", or "one glove, two gloves".

MATCH IT UP ... Sorting into groups is a key maths skill. Try jumbling up some socks then matching the pairs, or perhaps looking for all the black ones or the spotty ones. Naming the categories will help your baby to recognise them and build your baby's vocabulary.

MAKE CHOICES ... Try letting your baby or toddler choose between two different-coloured tops when getting dressed. Say how much you like their choice and why. Simple choices help to give your baby a sense of having some control over events.

In the Kitchen

HOW MANY? ... Talk to your baby as you lay the table. Count place settings out loud or ask your toddler to lay a spoon for each person and help them count them. Say "yours" and "mine" to help your baby's growing sense of identity. Mentioning numbers in practical contexts – how many segments of orange, how many plates? – familiarises your baby with their names and order.

DESCRIBING FOOD ... Mealtimes are a feast for the senses. Try talking about textures – soft pasta, crumbly bread; how food looks – bumpy broccoli, stringy spaghetti; how it smells – fruity, fishy; how it tastes – sweet, spicy; and what it sounds like – crunchy carrots, slurpy soup. All of these words build your baby's vocabulary and encourage them to use all their senses to explore.

GROWING COORDINATION ... Meal or snack times are a great opportunity for your baby to practise their hand–eye coordination skills. If they are ready, offer finger foods. Stay close by to supervise as they explore, and sometimes eat, these interesting new foods. A small spoon or fork will also develop dexterity and coordination.

At the supermarket

HIGH AND LOW ... Talk to your baby about what you're buying. Pointing out how some items are up high and others are down low helps your baby put this positional language into context.

WEIGHTS, MEASURES, NUMBERS ... A shopping trip is full of maths! You can count the apples, point out numbers on packages, and chat about what is heavy and what is light.

LITTLE HELPER ... Back home, try making a game out of emptying the shopping bags, naming each item as you take it out. You can talk about how to fit all the items in the cupboard to model problem-solving and even ask your toddler to help you find a place for each one.

In the park

HOW THINGS MOVE ... Point out how the trees move in the wind. Using descriptive words such as "swaying", "gusts" and "rustling" builds vocabulary and connects words to actions.

NATURE TRAIL ... Collect a treasure trove of items from the park to explore together. Look at leaves, twigs or a blade of grass and talk about how they look, feel and smell.

Nappy time

PEEKABOO ... Inject some fun into nappy-changing time. Use a clean muslin, your baby's vest or a blanket to hide your face. Say "Where's Mummy/Daddy?" then say "peekaboo" as you reveal your face. Your baby might be happy to play this time and again, building their understanding that you are there even when hidden.

TICKLE ME ... Use a muslin to tickle your baby's tummy or toes, saying "Tickle, tickle" before making contact. If you do this a few times, your baby may soon giggle in anticipation, learning that events can have an order.

Out and about

SHAPES AND WORDS ... On outings, keep an eye out for the shapes that are all around us. Point out round wheels, square windows and triangular road signs. Point out letters, words and numbers on posters, road signs and at stations.

COUNTING GAMES ... Count how many people are in the queue or how many stairs you and your toddler climb.

LISTEN OUT ... Keep an ear out for noises. If you hear a siren, a plane, or birdsong, mention these sounds so your baby learns to identify them. The ability to pick out sounds is a skill needed in learning to talk and, later, to read.

Bathtime

SPLISH SPLASH … Splash water, squeeze out a sponge, or explore bristles on a toothbrush. All of these activities and objects will help your baby explore textures, and understand how water behaves.

FILL IT UP … Let your baby play with empty containers in the bath. Fill them with water then pour it out. See what sinks and what floats to introduce these early science concepts.

WHO'S THAT? … Look in the bathroom mirror. Touch your baby's nose so they learn about parts of the body and build their self-awareness.

Bedtime

WHAT'S NEXT? … Understanding that events have an order reassures your baby and also helps them to grasp concepts such as patterns and sequences. Talk to your baby about their bedtime routine, "After bathtime we'll read a story then brush our teeth.".

Playtime

WHICH ONE? … Make a treasure box of recycled household objects such as cleaned yogurt pots, scrunchy food packets, paintbrushes and other safe objects. Supervise your baby while they explore the box but try to resist directing your baby's play – simply be ready to step in if invited or help is needed. Recognizing that there isn't a right or wrong way for your baby to play helps you to relax and allows them to choose which item to explore, which in turn builds your baby's confidence in making their own choices.

STORY TIME

Learning

through stories

As well as giving your baby a great start in learning to listen, talk, read and write, story time is full of fun and cuddles, helping you strengthen your bond. The best way to help your baby enjoy books and become a confident reader is to share lots of stories when they are very young. Lead by example, too. Your baby notices everything you do. If your baby sees you reading, for pleasure or a reason, such as looking at a recipe, they learn that reading is enjoyable and useful. Discover here how books can help your baby and use the ideas in this chapter to guide you when looking at books together.

Let's have story time...

When you share books, you are modelling the skills needed to read, such as turning pages. Follow the tips here to get started.

1 START EARLY ... It is never too soon to read to your baby. In the womb, babies hear from around 18 weeks. By 26 weeks, they respond to noises and voices. The first voice a baby comes to know is its mother's and the people she spends time with. It might feel strange, but you can talk and read to your baby before the birth.

2 THE RIGHT DISTANCE ... Newborn babies can focus only about 25cm away – about the distance from your face to theirs when you hold them in the crook of your arm. Hold books at this distance to help your baby see the pictures. As vision develops over the months, babies begin to judge distances and reach out to touch and explore books.

3 REPEAT, REPEAT ... You will soon find out which books are your baby's favourites. You can share these as often as you like as babies love to hear the same books again and again.

4 TIMING ... Sometimes your baby won't be in the mood for a book. They might be tired or hungry and may push the book away. Notice your baby's cues and try again another time.

5 MAKE IT UP ... Feel free to change some, or all, of the words in a story. The shared nature of the interactions between you and your baby are the most important thing. If books have no words, let your imagination lead you! You can cuddle up together and share books, chatting about pictures and making up stories to go with them.

Time to read

Sharing a book or story with babies or children once a day has been found to have a positive effect on overall development, including early communication, language and mental health. Discover how sharing books nurtures your baby in so many ways.

Language development

VOCABULARY ... Books expose your baby to lots of new words and connect words to objects, experiences and feelings. You can help your baby's understanding by pointing to and naming things on a page. Add sounds, such as "brumm brumm" as you point to a car to add to the fun and link words to pictures. Use your voice and body language, too, to reinforce concepts such as big, small, quiet or loud. All of this increases your baby's vocabulary, which in turn improves cognitive skills and lays the foundation for doing well at school later on. Don't worry if words or thoughts seem beyond your baby's understanding. Immersing your baby in language and ideas is the best possible start for them.

LEARNING TO LISTEN ... Story time helps babies to listen and pick out voices from background noise. Sharing books, even before babies understand words, introduces language, helping them learn to talk and, one day, read and write.

THE RHYTHM OF SPEECH ... Rhymes help babies tune in to the sounds and rhythms of speech, encouraging them to babble in their special "baby talk". One day, your baby will surprise you by saying a word you recognise (or something similar!), maybe filling a pause you left in a familiar rhyme or phrase.

Feelings and emotions

STRONG BONDS ... Story time is a wonderful opportunity for babies to experience two favourite things – being held close and hearing your voice. Reading out loud, or talking about pictures, is relaxing for you both. Your baby will come to associate books with the warmth and security they feel when cuddled up with you.

EXPLORING EMOTIONS ... Sharing stories helps your baby begin to understand and express feelings and learn about others' feelings – the start of empathy. Comment on characters' emotions. Do they look sad or happy? Are they laughing or crying? Communicate emotions through your own voice and facial expressions.

Pictures and numbers

COLOURS AND NUMBERS ... Babies can learn about shapes, numbers and colours in books. They are particularly drawn to contrasting colours and patterns. Some books focus on one theme, but you can point out these concepts in any book you look at.

Interaction

GETTING INVOLVED ... Recognise your baby's contributions. Leave gaps when you read so your baby has the chance to join in. You might notice your baby respond by waving their arms and kicking their legs or staring intently at the pictures. Or your baby might smile, laugh or point out something on the page.

SENSORY EXPLORATION ... Many books for babies can be explored with all the senses. Books made from sturdy board, vinyl or fabric can be mouthed, handled and dropped. Offer your baby books with textures, shapes, mirrors, flaps or holes, or books that make a noise. Investigating books helps your baby develop the manual dexterity needed to hold a book and turn its pages, and also to learn how to follow words across a page.

Stories with . . .

Movement

Books are a great way to explore movement and think about concepts such as speed (fast, slow); how things move (a brush sweeps, a wheel rolls); and how they change position (moving up and down or side to side). Notice how movement is woven into books and use words such as "whoosh" and "zoom" to convey these actions.

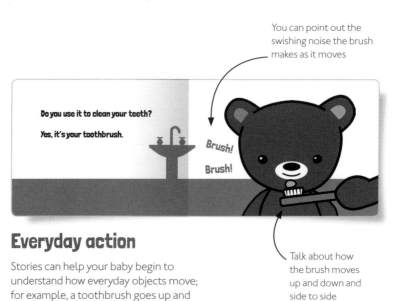

You can point out the swishing noise the brush makes as it moves

Do you use it to clean your teeth?

Yes, it's your toothbrush.

Brush!

Brush!

Talk about how the brush moves up and down and side to side

Everyday action

Stories can help your baby begin to understand how everyday objects move; for example, a toothbrush goes up and down or a spoon stirs round and round.

Baby Bear can see something green.

All types of transport

Different types of transport fascinate babies and help them understand how vehicles move. Draw your baby's attention to planes, boats, trains and tractors in books. As well as talking about colours and shapes, describe how they zoom through the air, bob on water or move along on wheels.

Point out how the round wheels help the green tractor move

Give extra emphasis to words that describe movement

Baby Bear and Dolly are on the swing.

Whee!

Fast and slow

Trace the movement with your finger

You could talk to your baby about how people, animals, or objects in stories are fast or slow. Is Baby Bear whizzing quickly down the slide? Look how slowly the tortoise is plodding along. Expressive words such as "whoosh", "whee" and "trudge" help to convey the sense of movement.

Stories with ...
Maths ideas

There is lots of early maths in children's books. Looking at books with your baby is a great way to help them build the skills and understanding they need to grasp a range of maths ideas, such as counting, shapes and position.

Point to the words for numbers to help your baby form a visual memory

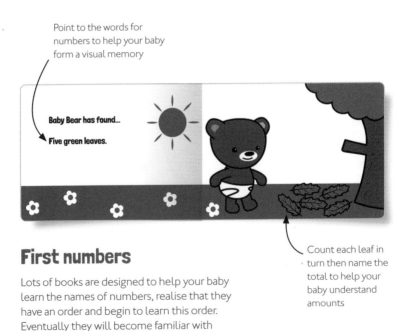

Baby Bear has found...

Five green leaves.

Count each leaf in turn then name the total to help your baby understand amounts

First numbers

Lots of books are designed to help your baby learn the names of numbers, realise that they have an order and begin to learn this order. Eventually they will become familiar with numbers and counting.

Now Baby Bear's had a drink,

Big Bear washes the cups in the sink.

Shapes and sizes

Point out different sizes and shapes. Point out, for example, how some cups are big and tall and some are small. Try tracing the outline of shapes with your finger as you say their name.

Talk about which is the biggest and smallest cup

Wonder out loud what is hiding "next to" Baby Bear

Can you guess what it is?

You wear it on your head when it's cold.

Point out positions

What's behind the flap? Who is next to the bear? Chat about the pictures. Hearing words about the position of something while you look at pictures together will help your baby begin to understand these mathematical ideas.

Look at what's "behind" the flap

Stories about...

Journeys

Story time helps your baby to explore familiar scenes and introduces them to exciting new worlds. Sharing books and stories with your baby will build their vocabulary, encourage their imagination and begin to teach them about the world beyond their experience.

Point out the different-coloured buckets and spades

Point to novel items such as seaweed to give your baby a visual image of the word

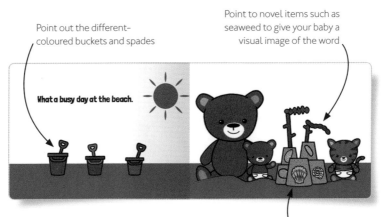

What a busy day at the beach.

New worlds

Has your baby been to the jungle or visited the seaside? They may not have seen a snake or felt the sand between their toes, but sharing stories is a wonderful way to introduce words that they might not hear in everyday conversation.

Shells and sandcastles may be new concepts to your baby

What a busy bus journey Baby Bear.

On the way

Stories can encourage your baby to think about journeys on buses and trains, or crossing the sea on a boat, or even taking a rocket to another planet. Talk about what you might see on the journey, such as cows in a field, the trees in the park, the fish in the sea – or the stars!

Talk about what Baby Bear can see out of the window

Chat about your baby's favourite activity at the park

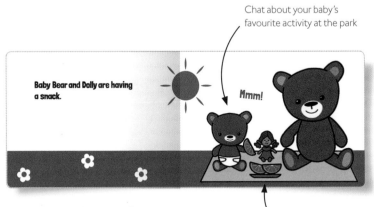

Baby Bear and Dolly are having a snack.

Mmm!

Going to the park

Stories about familiar places and scenes can be comforting, reminding babies of a familiar person or routine. A story about a visit to the park, for example, is a great opportunity to talk about a recent trip there and shows your baby that stories are interactive, triggering ideas and conversations with you.

Talk about what you saw and heard at the park on a recent trip

Stories with . . .

Noises

Stories can be full of noises, whether it's the siren of a fire engine, the rustling and swishing of trees in a breeze or the sounds animals make. Pointing out noises helps your baby learn to identify them, understand where different noises come from and think about concepts such as loud and quiet.

Point to the word for the noise an animal makes

Baby Bear can hear toy mouse behind the cardboard box.

Peek-a-boo!

Squeak!

Squeak!

Have fun making the noise yourself

Animal noises

Lots of children's stories are based around animals. As well as an animal's appearance, babies start to identify animals by the noises they make. Use books with animal characters to teach your baby about these different noises.

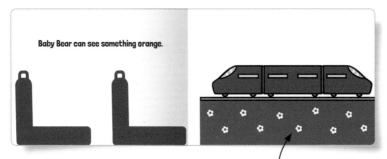

Baby Bear can see something orange.

Vehicle noises

Your baby may have heard the noise of a fire engine, bus, car or plane but not understood what the noise was. Seeing vehicles in books and talking about the noises they make helps your baby to put these noises into context.

Think about how to describe noises, such as the roar of an engine

A sponge in the orange paint.

Squelch!
Squelch!

Descriptive words

Words that mimic a noise will delight your baby, and are a great way to embed noises and words in your baby's mind. Talk about the swish of the paintbrush, the squelch of paint or the whoosh of the ribbons as they fly in the wind.

Babies love words that sound like the noise they describe

Stories with . . .

Characters

Story books introduce your baby to a world of new and exciting characters. These might be animals, people or even objects. Exploring how these characters look, what they do and say and how they feel helps your baby to learn about feelings and relationships.

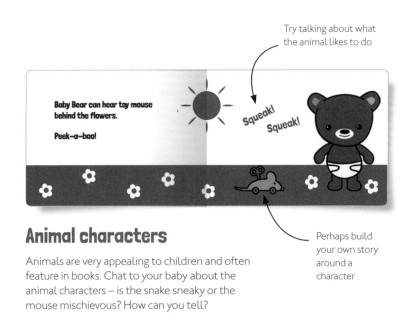

Try talking about what the animal likes to do

Baby Bear can hear toy mouse behind the flowers.

Peek–a–boo!

Squeak!
Squeak!

Animal characters

Animals are very appealing to children and often feature in books. Chat to your baby about the animal characters – is the snake sneaky or the mouse mischievous? How can you tell?

Perhaps build your own story around a character

Can you see Baby Bear wearing shiny sunglasses?

Talk about where Baby Bear might be going in sunglasses – on a train to the seaside maybe?

How characters look

Describing what an animal or person is wearing or what they look like helps your baby to understand that appearance can offer a clue as to what a character might be doing. For example, a uniform tells your baby about a character's occupation, or their outfit can reveal where they are going.

Point out how Baby Bear and Big Bear are smiling, happy to be at the park

Baby Bear and Dolly are at the park.

Learning about emotions

Stories are a great way to explore feelings. Your older baby or toddler is starting to understand basic emotions such as happy and sad, so pointing out characters' expressions, or reading a description of how a character feels and conveying the emotions in your voice reinforces these concepts. Over time this will help your child develop empathy and emotional understanding.

Opportunities...

For storytelling ... *When in a receptive mood, babies are ready for a story any time, any place and love to hear favourite stories again and again. As well as the traditional bedtime story, there are plenty of other ways to build stories – whether from books or made up – into your daily life.*

At home

THE BEDTIME STORY ... Babies and toddlers often love to be read a book at bedtime. This relaxed, end-of-day moment is the perfect time for you to capture some quiet time together. Your baby will relish snuggling up and receiving all your attention while enjoying a favourite book, or listening to a story you've made up. Let your imagination take over if you like or feel free to embellish a story. This special time will form a cherished part of your baby's daily routine. **MEALTIME TALES ...** You could try keeping your baby engaged at mealtimes by making up a story. It might be about who is coming to tea and what they would like to eat, or a story based around the items on the table – perhaps using different-sized bowls to tell your baby about Goldilocks and the three bears.

Out and about

ON THE MOVE ... Waiting at the bus stop or travelling on a bus or train are perfect times to look at a colourful storybook with your baby. It's a good idea to carry a book with you when you're away from home, or simply make up a story about your journey. Try adding in the people and places you see along the way. The story can be as silly as you like or quite simple, either way your baby will simply love to listen to your voice.
IN THE CAR ... Audio books come into their own on car journeys with babies, toddlers and children. Or you could record yourself reading a story and play this while travelling.

Library outing

BROWSE AND BORROW ... Joining a local library where available is a fantastic thing to do with your baby and you can enjoy a regular outing to the library together. Libraries are always happy for you to spend plenty of time there simply browsing, looking at stories and pictures together. Once you've joined up, help your baby pick a couple of favourite books to borrow and take home.
STORY TIME CLUBS ... Lots of libraries have story-time sessions for babies and toddlers, where stories and rhymes are read out loud in a group setting. Check what's on offer and take your baby along to encourage their love of storytelling and also help them to enjoy being in a social gathering.

Home-made books

REAL-LIFE STORIES ... Looking through the family photo album with your baby can be rewarding for you both. You can talk to your baby about their family history and give them a sense of their heritage. Talk, too, about events documented in the album and the emotions people are showing – for example, how happy everyone looked at a birthday party.

MAKE A SCRAPBOOK ... You could stick in souvenirs gathered from trips and days out as well as photos of family, friends and favourite scenes. Look through it together and chat about what you can see.

GET CREATIVE ... Have fun folding and cutting paper to create your own mini book together. Your older baby or toddler might want to make marks on the pages. Or cut out pictures from magazines and papers to stick in and look through with your baby. Show your baby how the book has a beginning, a middle and an end to help them begin to understand how books are read.

Create an adventure

Turn everyday trips to the supermarket or visits to the park into exciting adventure tales with your toddler as the star character. You could pretend they are a superhero, whizzing around in the supermarket trolley, or that you're trekking through the jungle as you walk through the park. All of these make-believe tales will feed their love of stories and show how imaginative storytelling can be woven into everyday life.

Story "prop" bag

Try making some story props. Choose one of your baby's favourite stories or rhymes and create some props from the story – for example, cut out a star and the moon for Twinkle, Twinkle, Little Star. Use your props along with the rhyme or song and watch for your baby's reaction. Can you tell if they are surprised, intrigued or delighted? Pop any small props into your bag – you never know when they might come in handy to amuse your baby.

Signs, logos and posters

Words are all around us. Point out words on street signs and logos and say these out loud so your baby learns that words are present in lots of different contexts and have a meaning. If you're feeling inspired, make a little story up using these words. Look at people and faces in posters and talk about how they look – do they seem happy or sad? Introduce your baby to these basic emotions and the concept of empathy, an important part of storytelling.

SONG TIME

Learning
through song time

Sharing songs and rhymes with your baby or toddler is a fantastic way to help every aspect of their development as well as enrich your relationship. Music helps us to develop bonds and feel an emotional connection with others. It is also linked to feelings, memory, language, creativity and learning, and brain imaging techniques are revealing how music fires connections between all of these areas in the brain. Discover exactly how song time benefits your baby and have fun sharing the action songs in this chapter together.

Let's sing...

Don't worry if you think you can't sing in tune – your baby won't mind and will definitely appreciate your efforts. Use the pointers below to get ready for song time.

1 **WOMB MUSIC ...** Musical experiences can start before birth. Babies are aware of the rhythmic sound of their mother's heart in the womb and soon hear external sounds. If you play music your baby may respond, becoming more, or less, active. You might notice a similar response after the birth.

2 **EXPRESS YOURSELF ...** It helps to talk to babies more slowly and in an expressive, high sing-song voice, known as parentese. This musical way of communicating helps your baby to feel secure, loved and close to you.

3 **HOLD HER CLOSE ...** Babies enjoy being gently rocked or gazing into your eyes as you sing or hum to them – you will probably find yourself swaying in time to the rhythm. Your baby watches the shape of your mouth as you sing and will learn to copy these shapes in their first vocalisations.

4 **BE PLAYFUL ...** Accompany songs with fun actions – walk your fingers up your baby's arm for Incy Wincy Spider, or blow a raspberry on your baby's tummy during a song. When in a receptive mood, your baby will love this interaction and will want to continue the fun, learning all the while.

5 **FOLLOW YOUR BABY'S CUE ...** Your baby will let you know if they aren't comfortable with an action song or not in the mood for a singalong. Follow your baby's cue and try again when they are in a receptive mood.

Time to sing

Action songs and rhymes encourage babies and toddlers to explore what their bodies can do and help learning in all sorts of ways.

On the move

BIG MOVEMENTS ... Rocking your baby to a lullaby or lifting or bouncing your baby to a lively song develops their sense of where their body is in "space". Songs that involve energetic actions, such as waving and moving the legs, develop balance and coordination and strengthen muscles, including those in the shoulders, arms and hands, which are needed to make marks and write. Actions crossing the body build brain connections to help coordinate both sides of the body.

HAND MOVEMENTS ... Songs that encourage small hand movements, known as fine motor control, strengthen and coordinate muscles in the hands and fingers. Eventually, these delicate movements will help your child tie laces or hold a pencil.

WATCHING YOU MOVE ... When you dance or move to words and music, your young baby will follow your movements with their eyes, strengthening eye muscles and improving focus.

Words and rhythm

LISTENING OUT ... As well as teaching your baby about rhythm and sounds, songs also encourage them to notice the rhythms of conversation and how to take turns to listen and respond. Repeating songs with memorable tunes also helps babies remember words more easily, especially when reinforced by actions, sounds or props. Over time, your baby will babble, coo, shriek and chuckle in response to songs, learning to control the mouth muscles needed to make sounds and form words.

Understanding

SELF-AWARENESS ... Babies love to hear their own name in a song. Acknowledge your baby with a touch or a cuddle as you say their name to develop self-awareness. You can also help your baby learn about their body by gently touching and naming features in songs such as Head, Shoulders, Knees and Toes.

STORIES AND EMOTIONS ... Like books, songs introduce words, ideas and stories, building your baby's understanding of the world and letting their imagination flourish. Songs also support babies' emerging awareness of feelings. Express emotions with your voice and body language when you sing to help this understanding.

Musical maths

NUMBERS AND MORE ... Songs and rhymes are fun ways to explore order, patterns, numbers, counting, shapes and size. As your baby learns a song, they become familiar with the names of numbers and eventually sing them in the song – a first step to realising that numbers have an order used for counting. Link actions to numbers, for example by counting on fingers or toes.

LEARNING ABOUT ORDER ... Babies may smile or wave excitedly when they recognise a song and know they are about to be lifted up or tickled! Your baby is developing a sense of order and knows what comes next, an understanding that helps with counting and more complex maths and science ideas later on. Pause before a word or action to let your baby join in with a sound, action, or roar of laughter!

MATHS WORDS ... Action songs are full of essential maths words such as ones to describe position (in, on, under); order (first, last); movement (fast, slow); direction (forwards, backwards); shape (round, square); or size (big, small).

Songs with . . .

Clapping

At The Baby Club, babies love joining in with the Clap Your Hands song. If you repeat the song two or three times, your baby may begin to anticipate the moment you tickle their tummy and giggle in gleeful expectation.

BODY AWARENESS

You can sing this song to the tune used at The Baby Club or a tune of your own. Do the actions and try saying the word "Now" very slowly to build the excitement before tickling your baby. As well as providing a sense of anticipation, Clap Your Hands teaches your baby about parts of their body – building vocabulary and self-awareness – and also develops coordination as your baby focuses on bringing their hands together to clap. Try finishing off with a soothing hug after all the action to signal the end of the song.

A HELPING HAND

Clapping is a skill your baby learns gradually. Start by guiding their hands together with your own so your baby gets the idea.

Clap Your Hands

Clap your hands, wiggle your toes,
stretch your arms, touch your nose.
Clap your hands, wiggle your toes,
stretch your arms, touch your nose.

Now...

Move your finger round your tummy,
Move your finger round your tummy...

Now...

Tickle, wiggle, tickle, wiggle!
Let's go again.

[Repeat all apart from the last line]

And end with a hug!

songs with . . .

Bouncing

The Bounce Together song is sung with a lively pace at The Baby Club. This fun song is a great way for babies to explore big movements – building muscle strength, improving coordination and developing spatial awareness as they move around.

FAST AND FUN

Sing this to the The Baby Club tune or make up your own, bouncing and wiggling your baby on your lap or holding your toddler's hands as they do the actions. You can use a scarf or just hands for the peekaboo verse. The repetitive movements combined with the element of surprise develop both muscle and visual memory, building brain pathways and teaching about movement and control.

BOUNCE AND WIGGLE

Bouncing up and down and wiggling side to side may challenge your baby. Go slowly at first and build the pace if your baby enjoys it.

Bounce Together

We bounce, bounce, bounce, bounce, bounce together,
We bounce, bounce, bounce, bounce, bounce together,
We bounce, bounce, bounce, bounce, bounce together,
Together is so much fun!

Next let's peekaboo...

We peek-a, peek-a, peek-a, peek-a-BOO together,
We peek-a, peek-a, peek-a, peek-a-BOO together,
We peek-a, peek-a, peek-a, peek-a-BOO together,
Together is so much fun!

Next we're gonna wiggle...

We wiggle, wiggle, wiggle, wiggle, wiggle together,
We wiggle, wiggle, wiggle, wiggle, wiggle together,
We wiggle, wiggle, wiggle, wiggle, wiggle together,
Together is so much fun!

Songs with...

Whispering

At The Baby Club, Baby Bear's Song alternates whispered verses with a lively chorus. As well as being fun, songs with this sort of dramatic effect encourage self-expression, build self-confidence and help your baby enjoy positive social interactions.

ADDING DRAMA

Whether to The Baby Club tune or your own, sing the verses very quietly, with a long, exaggerated "shhh", widening your eyes as you put a finger to your lips. Then spring into action with each chorus, helping your baby with the movement. The transition from still and quiet to active and noisy teaches your baby about these concepts.

"SHHH"

Songs that are quiet and noisy help your baby understand that there are times when it's fine to be noisy and others when being quiet is appropriate.

Baby Bear's Song

Baby Bear is quiet. Shhh.
Can you be quiet too? Shhh.
Baby Bear is quiet. (Hmmm...)
What's he going to do?

He's gonna jump, jump, jump, jump, jump!
He's gonna jump, jump, jump, jump, jump!
He's gonna jump, jump, jump, jump, jump!
Can you jump like Baby Bear?

Baby Bear is quiet. Shhh.
Can you be quiet too? Shhh.
Baby Bear is quiet. (I wonder...)
What's he going to do?

He's gonna clap, clap, clap, clap, clap!
He's gonna clap, clap, clap, clap, clap!
He's gonna clap, clap, clap, clap, clap!
Can you clap like Baby Bear?

Baby Bear is quiet. Shhh.
Can you be quiet too? Shhh.
Baby Bear is quiet. (Hmmm...)
What's he going to do?

He's gonna wiggle, wiggle, wiggle, wiggle, wiggle!
He's gonna wiggle, wiggle, wiggle, wiggle, wiggle!
He's gonna wiggle, wiggle, wiggle, wiggle, wiggle!
Can you wiggle like Baby Bear?

Songs with . . .

Swaying

Some songs with actions and movement can also be quiet and soothing, perfect for moments when you want to bring the energy down and give your baby some calm time. As you snuggle up to sing Twinkle, Twinkle Little Star, your baby will feel loved and secure.

SWAYING TOGETHER

Hold your baby and gently sway together as you sing this popular rhyme or make eye contact as your baby lies down or sits opposite you while you make a diamond shape with your fingers. You may find your older baby or toddler copies you in an attempt to make a diamond shape and may sway their body in time with the song.

CLEVER HAND SHAPES

Creating a diamond shape with the fingers is a feat of hand–eye coordination for your baby. Celebrate their efforts.

Twinkle, Twinkle Little Star

Twinkle, twinkle little star,
How I wonder what you are?
Up above the world so high,
Like a diamond in the sky.

When the blazing sun is gone,
When he nothing shines upon,
Then you show your little light,
Twinkle, twinkle all the night.

Then the traveller in the dark,
Thanks you for your tiny spark,
He could not see which way to go,
If you did not twinkle so.

In the dark blue sky you keep,
And often through my curtains peep,
For you never shut your eye,
'Till the sun is in the sky.

As your bright and tiny spark
Lights the traveller in the dark,
Though I know not what you are –
twinkle, twinkle little star.

Songs with . . .

Pointing

An engaging rhyme, Wind the Bobbin Up has a whole range of learning opportunities. As well as introducing the skill of pointing, this simple song includes numbers and positional language, builds vocabulary and develops coordination.

ACT IT OUT

Sing this song at a moderate, steady pace so your baby can absorb the words and join in with all the actions when ready. The short phrases and repetition in the verses will help your baby to remember the words and numbers, ready to recall another time. Your older baby may start to copy you as you model pointing, giving them a valuable non-verbal communication tool.

POINT IT OUT

Pointing is an exciting development for babies, providing an easy way to make their needs known. Be sure to pay attention!

Wind the Bobbin Up

Wind the bobbin up,
Wind the bobbin up,
Pull, pull, clap, clap, clap.
Wind it back again,
Wind it back again,
Pull, pull, clap, clap, clap.

Point to the ceiling,
Point to the floor,
Point to the window,
Point to the door.
Clap your hands together, one, two, three,
Put your hands upon your knee.

Wind the bobbin up,
Wind the bobbin up,
Pull, pull, clap, clap, clap.
Wind it back again,
Wind it back again,
Pull, pull, clap, clap, clap.

Point to the ceiling,
Point to the floor,
Point to the window,
Point to the door,
Clap your hands together, one, two, three,
Put your hands upon your knee.

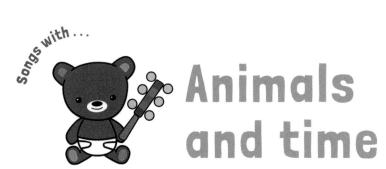

Songs with . . .

Animals and time

A simple, fast-paced rhyme, Hickory Dickory Dock teaches your baby about the rhythms of language and explores ideas such as movement, position and time. Babies love songs with animals and these help your baby to visualise the actions of the animals.

UP AND DOWN

Try running your fingers up and down your baby's body as you sing this rhyme, or encourage your older baby to copy the actions of fingers running up and down. This helps your baby to build the small muscles in the hand and master more refined movements. The song also helps your baby to experience lots of maths ideas and language as they have fun hearing about numbers, time, positional language and sequences.

Hickory Dickory Dock

Hickory, dickory, dock,
The mouse ran up the clock.
The clock struck one,
The mouse ran down,
Hickory, dickory, dock.

(Repeat)

Hickory, dickory, dock,
The mouse ran up the clock.
The clock struck one,
The mouse ran down,
Hickory, dickory, dock.

THINKING ABOUT TIME

It will be a while before your baby can tell the time, but songs that mention time introduce the general concept to your baby.

Songs with . . .

1
2
3
Counting

Nursery rhymes and songs such as Five in the Bed that are built around numbers are a great way to introduce your baby to early maths, helping them discover that numbers have a set order and introducing the concept of counting.

COUNTING BACKWARDS

Hold the corresponding number of fingers up for each verse as you sing this song with your baby, and make a rolling action with your hands. Counting down from five shows your baby that numbers can be counted backwards as well as forwards, but are always in the same sequence. Removing a number with each verse also introduces the idea of subtraction.

MAKE IT REAL

To bring this song to life, you could gather five of your baby's soft toys and roll these off the bed one by one.

Five in the Bed

There were five in the bed
And the little one said,
"Roll over! Roll over!"
So they all rolled over and one fell out.

There were four in the bed
And the little one said,
"Roll over! Roll over!"
So they all rolled over and one fell out.

There were three in the bed
And the little one said,
"Roll over! Roll over!"
So they all rolled over and one fell out.

There were two in the bed
And the little one said,
"Roll over! Roll over!"
So they all rolled over and one fell out.

There was one in the bed
And the little one said,
"Good night!"

Opportunities...

For song time ... *Bringing music into routines is a great way to enjoy positive interactions while also helping your baby develop listening and social skills and build coordination and vocabulary. Use the ideas here to add music and joy to your baby's day.*

Changed and ready

NAPPY TIME ... Nappy time involves lots of eye-to-eye contact so is a great time to sing a song. Songs that incorporate parts of the body, such as Head, Shoulders, Knees and Toes are perfect as you can point to the parts of the body. Your older baby might join in and point to the parts of their face when these are named.

GETTING DRESSED ... A made-up "getting dressed" song can help this often tricky task go smoothly. Include verses on popping on a vest, putting your arms and legs through and doing up buttons.

End of the day

BATHTIME FUN ... Singing during bathtime is lots of fun. You can sing songs about ducks or sailing on the sea, perhaps making up some actions, such as pretending your hand is a boat bobbing along. Your older baby or toddler may join in or simply enjoy listening.

BEDTIME LULLABY ... This is the time when you want your baby to relax so energetic songs aren't ideal. Instead, sway your baby to a soothing lullaby to calm them and get them ready for sleep.

On the move

CAR JOURNEY SING-ALONG ... Play some gentle nursery rhymes or favourite children's songs in the car to sing along to. Choose familiar songs so your older baby or toddler can do some of the actions while you drive, or join in if you're a passenger.

WALKING SONGS ... Sing a marching song such as The Grand Old Duke of York as you walk along with your toddler. You may not get far, but this is a great way to encourage your little one to practise their walking skills.

Tune in

ON THE RADIO ... Have the radio on so you can enjoy a dance with your baby when a lively song is played. Cuddle your baby and sway around the room, or hold your toddler's hands while they jump up and down enthusiastically to the music.

TV TUNES ... There are plenty of ditties and songs on television, even in commercial breaks. If there is one you both really enjoy, have a go at making up simple actions to go with the words.

Active playtime

SONGS WITH CHARACTERS ... Enjoy some pretend play with your baby by singing songs that involve their favourite toys. You can bounce your baby and a favourite teddy up and down as you sing Teddy Bear's Picnic, or sing songs about trains, buses or toy animals, making the actions as you sing.

USING PROPS ... Find a light scarf or some ribbons and wave these around with your baby, singing a song in time with the actions.

WINDING DOWN

Learning
through calm time

As The Baby Club draws to a close, part of the routine is for babies to enjoy some calm time to help wind down after playtime, stories and songs. In the programme, bubbles are gently blown to signal a change in pace and that it will soon be time to say goodbye. Other soothing activities, such as sharing books and stories, singing gentle songs and tidying away also help babies to feel calm. Try the ideas in this chapter to enjoy calm time together and discover how these activities can also help your baby's learning and development.

Let's wind down...

After an energetic time playing, enjoying stories, and singing, the tips below can help you get ready for some calm time together.

1 **MODEL CALM TIME ...** Your baby is sensitive to your mood and often responds by matching their mood to yours. While it's not always easy to wind down, especially when tired, try to take a moment to sit together and, for example, notice the beautiful bubbles, share a story or slow your breathing in time with some music. If you feel relaxed, your baby is more likely to relax with you.

2 **AVOID DISTRACTIONS ...** Turn off the TV or a loud radio and put your phone on silent and out of sight, so you and your baby can enjoy winding down without interruptions.

3 **SPEAK SOFTLY ...** Adjust your voice to match the mood. Talk quietly and calmly to indicate a slower pace and show your baby that this is a time for quiet, gentle activity.

4 **MAKE IT FAMILIAR ...** Creating routines around winding down, where activities happen in a familiar, predictable order, helps your baby to understand what's happening. Babies and young children quickly learn what is coming next and this helps them to feel safe and secure.

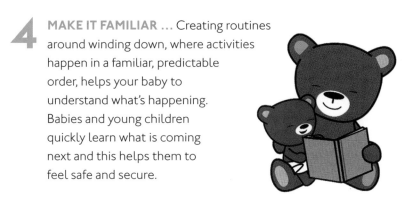

Time to wind down

Calming activities are ideal at times of the day when you want to slow the pace. These soothing activities also have other developmental benefits for your baby.

Bubble time

MOUTH MOVEMENTS ... Babies are entranced by bubbles and how they appear as if by magic. Relaxing to watch, bubbles also help babies to practise the mouth movements needed to talk. If you sit or lay your baby down so they can see your face, they might watch intently as you puff out your cheeks, blow gently and conjure up a bubble. Try exaggerating your mouth movements so they can clearly see these. Pause to see how your baby responds. They might not copy you straight away, waiting instead to be invited by an encouraging look or smile from you. Perhaps they will try to copy the shape of your mouth or cheeks. This helps them practise the tongue and mouth movements needed to form words.

Slightly older babies may try to blow bubbles themselves. Eventually they learn how to control their chest and mouth muscles, and work out how much breath is needed to blow a bubble, helping them get ready to talk and sing.

COORDINATION ... Blowing bubbles is a perfect opportunity for practising hand–eye coordination. When your baby holds the wand and tries to dip it into the bubble mixture, they are developing their grip – the first stage in learning to hold a pencil and write.

CAUSE AND EFFECT ... As your baby plays, they realise that they can pop the bubbles! This helps them understand how they can affect the world around them.

Songs and stories

SNUGGLING UP ... Listening to lullabies and gentle music while being held close, or snuggling up for a story are both very calming for your baby and also help to strengthen your bond. Repeated melodies and swaying rhythms are soothing and reassuring.

Making marks

DOODLE AWAY ... Older toddlers may find time spent sitting with you quietly doodling with crayons soothing and restful after energetic play. Chatting about the marks your baby makes helps them start to understand how their marks can have a meaning.

Time outside

BEING OUTDOORS ... Taking your baby for a stroll in their buggy, perhaps on a trip to the park, allows them to enjoy some fresh air and creates a restful moment in your baby's day. Being outside in nature has widely recognised benefits, helping to soothe the mind and providing physical stimulus that in turn has a calming effect.

Tidy up time

TIDYING UP ... Putting objects and toys away can become an important part of your baby's routine, helping them accept that playtime is over and understand that they will return to it later or on another day. If your older baby or toddler helps you tidy up, this is also great practise for their hand–eye coordination. Chat about what you're doing or even try singing a tidy up song.

Poem time...

Bubbles

At The Baby Club, playtime, story time and lively songs are followed by some gentle bubble time to help the babies wind down after all the activity and fun. As well as enjoying watching the bubbles on the programme with your baby, you could try blowing some at home, or try other calming activities to help your baby wind down.

CALMING BUBBLES ... Bubbles often entrance babies and can be both stimulating and calming. When using bubbles to help calm your baby, use a gentle, soothing voice. Echo your baby's amazement at the bubbles and give your older baby a go at blowing one. Think about your facial expression, too. Seeing pleasure on your face reassures your baby that bubbles, though unusual, are exciting and not at all scary. Chat about how bubbles float and pop and perhaps try to capture one as it floats past.

Pointing ...

The Bubble poem

Bubbles drifting through the air.
Some pop here, some pop there.

Watch the bubbles floating high.
Off they drift into the sky.

One, two, three, four,
Now it's time to blow some more.

Blow the bubbles high and low.
Off they float, where will they go?

watching . . .

. . . catching

Tidy up time

Tidying up after playtime, putting objects back in the bag or toys back in a basket, is part of the wind-down routine at The Baby Club. Getting your baby involved in tidying away helps to signal that playtime is over for now, to be returned to either later or on another day.

TIDYING UP TOGETHER ... Chatting calmly to your baby about what you are doing while tidying away engages your baby in this wind-down activity. You could mention how much fun you've both had exploring, singing and reading together while you tidy away and how you both can look forward to the next playtime. This natural conclusion to your baby's play becomes part of your baby's routine, a predictable and reassuring part of their day.

> When we started to put the object back in the bag, I thought she might cry, but she surprised me. She put it away happily as she knew playtime was over and it was time to go home.
>
> *Kate, Ruby's mum*

Opportunities...

For winding down ...Exploring the world is very stimulating for your baby, and their energy levels and attention span will naturally go up and down during the day – as will yours! Having some calm time will help you both recharge your batteries. The ideas here can help you incorporate calming activities into your day.

Bubble time

MAGIC BUBBLES ... Bathtime is a perfect moment to enjoy blowing bubbles with your baby and can be a magical part of your baby's wind-down routine. Or try blowing bubbles outside, in the park or, if you have outside space, in the garden. Sitting on grass, blowing bubbles and watching these float on the breeze, can be incredibly relaxing.

Colouring time

DOODLES AND MARKS ... If your toddler enjoys making marks, get out some paper and crayons and sit with them while they scribble away. Chat quietly about the patterns they are making and the colours they have used. This gentle activity can be a great way to transition from livelier, active play, perhaps calming your little one before a meal or in the run up to their bedtime routine.

A change of scene

TAKING A WALK ... Taking your baby out in the buggy or having a short walk with your toddler, whether in the park or even just to the shops, can create a restful moment in the day. The change of scene and welcome fresh air allow you both to enjoy some quiet time without activities and games.

ENJOYING NATURE ... Being in nature can soothe babies and adults alike. A trip to the park – seeing the ducks, feeling the grass and enjoying the breeze – can calm your baby. Chat about what you can see – perhaps point out clouds or how the sunlight dapples through the leaves.

Stories and songs

SHARING STORIES ... You can cuddle up for a story at any time, but there are moments when this can be especially calming. Try sharing a story after a busy playtime or before a meal and, of course, at bedtime to create a quiet, calm mood.

SOOTHING LULLABIES ... Try singing a gentle song or listening to some rhythmic music on car journeys, at bathtime, or at bedtime. A soothing lullaby can also be helpful if your baby is overtired and fractious and simply needs to be held close, listening to your voice.

Tidying away

ALL IN ORDER ... Quiet tidy up time can be a regular feature of your baby's day. As well as tidying up toys after playtime, tidy away picnics, after meals, and put clothes away at the end of the day. This helps your baby adjust to the ebbs and flow of the day and provides a reassuring sequence to events.

GOODBYE

Learning
through saying goodbye

Goodbye and thank you for joining in with The Baby Club. Like The Hello Song on page 15, The Goodbye Song on page 185 is part of the routine of The Baby Club. Singing goodbye lets everyone know that the group is coming to an end and that it is soon time to leave, creating a familiar, reassuring routine for babies.

We hope that you and your baby have enjoyed playing together and learning through exploring everyday objects, singing and reading stories.

Feeling secure

REGULAR ROUTINES ... Routines provide comfort and security for babies and young children and can be particularly helpful when there are changes happening in their lives, such as when moving house, starting nursery or when there is a new arrival in the family. They are also helpful when someone else looks after your baby.

Including songs such as The Goodbye Song in everyday routines helps to reinforce what is happening and convey whether it is a time to be lively and active or quiet and still. The Goodbye Song in The Baby Club is gentle and quiet, giving parents and carers a chance to snuggle up with their little ones and reflect on all the fun they have had together.

Actions and words

REINFORCING MEANING ... The combination of seeing, doing and hearing is the best possible way to help your baby learn and understand words and language. Singing The Goodbye Song is a lovely way to help your baby link the action of waving to the word "goodbye" and to understand the meaning of waving.

THE ART OF COPYING ... Your baby learns how to wave by copying you. If you are watching The Baby Club together, wave to Baby Bear or Baby Tiger, saying "Bye bye, see you again soon!". Make a habit of waving to friends and family, too, to characters in books and even to objects as you put them back in the bag for another day. You might find that your baby waves to say goodbye or just when they are ready to do something else. It is just one of the many ways your baby will find to communicate feelings before being able to speak.

BUILDING RESILIENCE ... Saying goodbye and waving are important to babies and young children because they help them to understand that someone is leaving but will be back again soon. This important lesson builds resilience and helps your baby to say goodbye without getting upset.

Song time...

Saying goodbye

The Baby Club draws to a gentle close with The Goodbye Song. As well as joining in while watching the programme, you might find it's fun to sing this song with your baby when saying goodbye to family and friends. Your baby will love the familiarity of the song and understand that it's time to say goodbye.

SNUGGLE UP AND SING ...
Hold your baby close and cuddle up together while you quietly sing or say The Goodbye Song. You might find your baby is already dropping off to sleep, or is happy just to rest in your arms after all the stimulating activities.

Cuddle . . .

The Goodbye Song

Goodbye, Baby Bear. We've had so much fun.
Goodbye to you too, we've giggled,
We've danced, we've sung.

Goodbye, friends, we'll see you another day.

Until next time...

Goodbye, everyone, come back soon to play!

Goodbye!

wave . . .

. . . and sleep

Come again

We hope you've enjoyed exploring all the ideas behind The Baby Club activities and finding out how these help your baby, and that you will continue to watch and join in with The Baby Club. You might also be encouraged to find out about and visit a baby club in your area.

FUN FOR ALL ... Watching The Baby Club or going to one in your area can become a much-looked-forward-to part of your baby's routine. As you get into a routine of going to a baby club, you can observe how babies of different ages interact – younger ones tending to play alongside rather than with each other, while older toddlers might start to interact more. For yourself, you may find that meeting other local parents allows you to exchange stories and advice and help you and your baby make some new friends!

"We started taking Theo to baby clubs from two months old and this has built his confidence over time ... he smiles at everyone."

Ara, Theo's mum

Index

Penguin
Random
House

Senior Editor Claire Cross
Senior Designer Alison Gardner
Designer Vanessa Hamilton
Editorial Assistant Kiron Gill
Jacket Designer Amy Cox
Jacket Coordinator Nicola Powling
Senior Producer, Pre-production Tony Phipps
Senior Producer Luca Bazzoli
Managing Editor Dawn Henderson
Managing Art Editor Marianne Markham
Art Director Maxine Pedliham
Publisher Mary-Clare Jerram

Consultant Editor Sally Smith EdD, CEO Peeple

The Baby Club television series was created by
Emma Hyman and Christopher Pilkington and
produced by David Hallam, Jon Hancock and
Tom O'Connell.

First published in Great Britain in 2020 by Dorling
Kindersley Limited, 80 Strand, London, WC2R 0RL

Copyright © 2020 Dorling Kindersley Limited
A Penguin Random House Company
10 9 8 7 6 5 4 3 2 1
001–316473–Feb/2020

A CIP catalogue record for this book is available
from the British Library.
ISBN: 978-0-2414-1021-9
Printed and bound in Latvia

Picture credits:
(Key: b-below/bottom; c-centre; l-left; r-right) **123RF.
com:** victoroancea 114; © **Dorling Kindersley:** 14(br), 19,
26, 27(l), 35(l), 43(l), 50, 51(l), 58, 59(l), 64 (b - hand), 65
(b - hand), 66, 67(l), 74, 75(l), 80 (b - feet), 82, 83(l), 90,
91(l), 96 (bl - paddle), 98, 99(l), 106, 107(l), 115(l), 120
(cb - teapot), 152(b), 156(b), 158(b), 160(b);
Dreamstime.com: Carlosphotos 34; **Icon made by
Freepik from** www.flaticon.com (baby icons).

All other images © **Three Arrows Media, Tiny House
Productions and CMP**

For further information see: www.dkimages.com
A world of ideas:
SEE ALL THERE IS TO KNOW
www.dk.com

Acknowledgments

The publisher would like to thank:
Sally Smith, CEO of Peeple, for her guidance,
words and support; Three Arrows production
company for their support and advice; and the
families who have taken part in The Baby Club.

Lucy Smith for photography
Claire Wedderburn-Maxwell for proofreading
Hilary Bird for the index

From Sally Smith, the Consultant Editor:
I would like to thank Helen Stroudley, Early
Years Consultant, Peeple, and Claire Cross, the
editor at DK, for all their help and advice, and to
acknowledge all the Peeple staff and colleagues
who contributed to the Peep Learning Together
Programme. Finally, I would like to thank my
children, Joss, Tristan and Meggie for helping
me learn, slowly, how to be a parent.

About Peeple

Peeple is a charity that supports parents and
children to make the most of the learning
opportunities in everyday activities. You probably
do lots of these activities already – Peeple
developed the Peep Learning Together
Programme to explain why they are so helpful.
Peeple are based in Oxford where they work with
local families and train practitioners from around
the UK and beyond to use their programme. They
are educational consultants for The Baby Club
and lots of Peep ideas are used in this book. Have
fun playing and learning together!

supporting parents and
children to learn together

Disclaimer
The publisher and author disclaim any
responsibility for injuries, accidents, or damages
resulting directly or indirectly from the games
and activities described and illustrated in this
book. Appropriate and reasonable supervision
of children at all times based on the age and
capability of the child is recommended.